The Northern Counties Cookbook

PHILIP ATKINSON

SISTER MOON PUBLICATIONS

DEDICATION

To the home cooks who feed tradition with nutrition and love. To families who make the time to sit down and eat together around the same table. To the people who sow it and grow it, harvest and process it. To honest preparation of homely food.

With thanks to Dave Preston for his editing expertise and to Simon Raine of the Weardale Cheese Company for advice on the cheese making section. And to Darlene Ross for the encouragement and countless cups of tea.

CONTENTS

FOREWORD

England's Northern Counties comprise the old counties of Northumberland, Durham, Cumberland, Westmorland and the North Riding of Yorkshire. It was once the heart of the ancient Kingdom of Northumbria and is an eclectic place of surprising contrasts: the stark Pennine Hills roll eastward down to heather-covered moorland, on to the fertile coastal plain and the bounty of the North Sea, and westward to the stunning Lake District and the Irish Sea. It's a land of forests, pastoral hills, farmland and lush meadows, cut through by salmon-run rivers with grayling, char, brown and sea-trout and under-utilized crayfish. In different ages, the land had different characteristics. Over the past two hundred years, the hills were animated with the coming and goings of lead miners, then left to the sheep, then rediscovered first by walking enthusiasts and then by curious tourists wishing to experience the countryside made famous by storytellers such as Beatrix Potter, James Herriot, Ann Cleeves and Catherine Cookson. Much of Northumberland, East Durham and South Yorkshire were covered for two centuries in abominable industrial waste and coal mines that for a long time defined the region and its people. In the 18th and 19th centuries, the industrial boom in the Northern Counties brought people to the area in numbers that far outstripped the more famous gold-rushes of North America. Cornish, Welsh and Irish flocked to join the omnipresent Scots and the indigenous English, themselves proud descendants of Britons, Romans and Vikings. And with the immigrants came the different tastes and customs that eventually flourished into one of the most interesting regional cookery traditions of Great Britain. It is good to see traditional recipes—updated and refined—that once were common are now making a comeback in the resurgence of fine cooking both at home and in the dining rooms of better restaurants throughout the Northern Counties.

I was prompted to write this book for several reasons, not least of which was that I'd been collecting regional recipes since I was a teenager, but the book notion came one evening while out to dinner at an expensive five-star restaurant. For a first course I chose *cônfit du canard*, served on a tower of *pommes au gratin* with *couleé orange*. It was smashing. Of course, I also knew it as potted duck with Pan Haggerty—if it had come with elderberry syrup instead of the orange sauce it would have been pure Northern Counties. Piqued by this curious parallel, I searched the menu for an entrée and discovered there were lots of choices similar to the dishes of home. Soup using leeks was there, even rabbit was back in vogue. Lamb, in particular, was offered in several ways, but what I had— though good—was not so good as the superb lamb grazed on the wild herbs and sweet grass of the Simonside Hills. Some of the *a la carte* vegetables were straight out of my mother's repertoire: baby carrots, braised red cabbage, celeriac, sorrel and spinach salad— even the mash sounded special when called *pommes purée*. I couldn't find an equivalent of Northern Counties country wine, but there was a fabulously expensive ice-wine reminiscent of Lindisfarne mead, only sweeter. The bill came to slightly more than I paid for my first car. But it was really, really good. And for the life of me I could not think of a good reason why Northern Counties recipes should not be allowed to shine in a similar manner.

Here, then, are some of the traditional recipes that once were common in homes all over the Northern Counties—it is not complete, and I am aware that many are known and enjoyed throughout the country, but it is good to see that so many are now making a comeback in the resurgence of fine cooking available in the dining rooms of the north's better restaurants.

A Brief History of The Ancient Kingdom of Northumbria

Our knowledge of the inhabitants of the British Isles before 2000 years ago is scant at best, but around that time, the islands were inhabited by closely-related Celtic peoples speaking dialects of British and Gaelic, organized somewhat in small tribal states. Across the central area of Great Britain, however—from the Scottish borders in the north as far south as modern Derbyshire— was Brigantia, the precursor of the Kingdom of Northumbria. Brigantia was named in honour of the Celtic goddess Brigant, who was worshipped right throughout the British Isles and became Christianized as St. Bridget.

The Romans invaded and subdued much of Britain 43 years into the Common Era. They built a city at Eboracum (modern York) and emasculated troublesome Brigantia by dividing it with the famous Hadrian's Wall—stretching almost coast to coast from Carlisle to Wallsend. When their empire began to collapse in the early fifth century, Rome recalled its soldiers from Britain to protect the capital. Coel Hen (Cole the Old, or Old King Cole) was king of the Scottish Lowlands and became king over much of northern and central Britain at the retreat of the Romans. Northern Britain reverted to its pre-Roman condition of small states ruled by princes for the next century.

After 573, the northern principalities were brought under the control of the kings of Bernicia, based at Bamburgh. At that time, most of the population spoke British (Welsh) but already people in the north east were adopting that mixture of Germanic, Welsh and Latin that was to become English. In 603, King Ethelfrith ruled a reunited land that stretched from the Humber to the Firth of Forth, renamed—in English—Northumbria.

Ethelfrith was followed by Edwin, who expanded the kingdom of Northumbria to its greatest extent. His seat of power and court were at Edinburgh (Edwin's borough). Edwin introduced an age of peace and learning that lasted two hundred years.

In the ninth century the Danes arrived. They annexed much of southern Northumbria, nowadays known as Yorkshire, renaming the Roman regional capital 'Jorvik' which is since glossed to York. When the West Saxons eventually defeated the Danes, they declared themselves overlords of Northumbria and one of them, Edward, sold the northern areas (Edinburgh and the Borders) to Scotland, ensuring that afterwards Northumbria would never again have the strength to be a serious military threat to the English or the Scots. This also ensured that Scotland would become an English speaking state—at that time ordinary Scots spoke British (Welsh or Pictish dialects) and the ruling classes spoke Gaelic. The western areas of Northumbria (modern Dumfries) had been part of Scotland for some time.

The Normans arrived in 1066, but after William's success at Hastings, the north backed the wrong side by inviting King Harald of Norway to lead them against the new king, for which they suffered 'the harrowing of the North.' The Normans killed ninety per cent of the population—including women and children—in South Durham and North Yorkshire.

Despite the genocide, the Normans never did quite manage to subdue the area completely, and when King Stephen took the throne of England the north stayed loyal to the Empress Matilda. It was not until the time of Henry II (1157) when the new castle was built (hence Newcastle upon Tyne), that the English gained full control over the north and the current Scottish border was agreed upon (Berwick upon Tweed changed hands as many as thirteen times before finally becoming part of England). Southern Northumbria was already known as Yorkshire; in the west new counties were created: Lancashire, Westmorland and Cumberland; Durham County became an autonomous palatinate under the Bishop of Durham to serve as a military buffer zone, and the remaining area took the name Northumberland.

A Note on Weights and Measures

When first I began to write down recipes they came in all manner of media: briefly spoken over a pint in the pub, scribbled hastily on a napkin, or translated from the notebooks of our elders. I struggled a bit as to what system to use. The old system of pounds and ounces was interspersed with common teacup measures and other more personal references (my mother used terms like 'knob', 'bit of' 'slack handful' 'pinch' and 'some' as though we'd all know exactly what she meant), so in the end I have gone the sensible route of using metric measurements. It's simple and reliable. Won't it be great when we finally all use the same system? Or perhaps not —perhaps the casualties of uniformity would be the quirks and eccentricities that make regional cookery worth exploring. I like to say, 'As you like it … the choice is yours.'

To be consistently successful in reproducing these old-fashioned but in the main simple recipes, I urge you to get to know your ingredients, your pots and pans, and especially your oven.

Some local specialities can be substituted:

Bilberries - blueberries
Dales cheese - Cheshire or Caerphilly
Durham Mustard - Dijon or similar
Mushroom ketchup - Worcestershire sauce
Rapeseed oil - Sunflower, vegetable or olive oil
Yorkshire Relish - half-and-half Worcestershire sauce/cider vinegar
Elderberry wine - dry red wine
Wild mushrooms - store-bought shiitake, ceps, oysters or morels

Oven temperature equivalents:

Celsius	Gas Mark	Descriptive	Fahrenheit
140 °C	1	Very Cool/Slow	285 °F
150 °C	2	Cool/Slow	300 °F
160 °C	3	Warm	320 °F
180 °C	4	Moderate	355 °F
190 °C	5	Moderate	375 °F
200 °C	6	Moderately Hot	390 °F
220 °C	7	Hot	430 °F
230 °C	8	Hot	450 °F
245 °C	9	Hot	475 °F
260 °C	10	Very Hot	500 °F

Serving sizes given are mostly suggestions.

Eggs are medium unless otherwise specified.

Use standard metric measuring spoons: tablespoon: 15ml, teaspoon: 5ml. A pinch is about what you can grab between your thumb and two forefingers, more or less.

Prague cures No.1 and No.2 are available from sausage makers and online and may be omitted if you're not sure how to use them.

SALADS

Salads in the Northern Counties were not traditionally served as they are these days—that is, basically leafy lettuce and dressing. They would always have had a protein as the central focus, often something as simple as a slice of pork pie or a piece of salmon or cheese, or often just sliced, hard-boiled eggs.

Goat Cheese, Beetroot and Apple Salad

When I was a boy I was scared stiff of the goat that was tethered to a patch of free grazing in our village. It would lower its head and have a run at anyone who came near, including the owner. Its owner kept it because she was lactose sensitive and the goat milk allowed her to have her tea as she liked it. I don't know if she made cheese, but for those who wish to try, recipes are on page 193.

- Mixed salad greens
- Sliced apple (dip slices in lemon juice to stop them going brown)
- Cooked sliced beetroot
- Walnuts or toasted pine nuts
- Goat cheese
- Cold-pressed rapeseed oil

- Lay a bed of dressed, mixed salad greens (lettuce, dandelion leaves, etc.) on each plate and add five wedges of apples like numbers on a clock face.
- Place pieces of beetroot between each piece of apple and sprinkle walnuts or toasted pine nuts over the top.
- Place a large mound of goat cheese in the centre and top with a piece of beetroot and a couple of pieces of walnut.
- Drizzle a little cold-pressed rapeseed oil over everything, a grind of black pepper, and serve.

Green Salad

A simple side salad to accompany any meal.

- Lettuce - 1 large head washed, dried and ripped to small pieces
- Spring onions - 6 chopped fine
- Mustard greens - handful
- Cress - handful
- Durham Salad Cream (page 4) - to coat

- Mix all the greens together and dress just before serving.

Spring Salad

An old-fashioned and pretty salad I remember from the meatless days of Lent during my childhood.

- Lettuce - 1 head leaves whole, washed, drained and dried
- Chives - small bunch snipped small
- Carrots - 3 raw and grated
- Beetroot - 3 boiled and sliced
- Dales cheese - 100g grated

- Cover a plate with the lettuce leaves.
- Pile the cheese in the centre.
- Place a ring of beetroot slices around the cheese.
- Sprinkle with chopped chives and serve.

Harperley Salad

If this were made with mozzarella instead of goat cheese you could call it 'insalata Caprese.' As it is, it often carries the more homely name of tomato and cheese salad. It does have a faint Italian provenance in that this recipe came from a Bishop Auckland woman who had the salad made for her in 1944 by an Italian soldier from the prisoner of war camp near Harperley Hall in the Wear Valley.

- Fresh, fresh tomatoes, sliced thick
- Goat cheese
- Basil oil (made by blending a bunch of fresh basil with some good safflower, cold-pressed rapeseed or light olive oil)
- Fresh basil leaves, shredded
- Salt & black pepper

- Arrange the slices of tomato alternatively with slices of cheese.
- Sprinkle with shredded basil and drizzle basil oil over the top.
- Add a grind of black pepper and some coarse sea salt and that's it
  —simplicity itself.

Potato Salad

Some people make a variation of this by adding chopped, crisp, bacon pieces.

- Potatoes - 500g boiled and cut into small dice
- Radishes - 6 washed and grated
- Durham Salad Cream - 100ml (below)
- Chives - a small bunch snipped small

- Mix the potato cubes while still warm with the dressing and the radishes. When cold, add the chives and serve immediately.

Northern Counties Ploughman's Lunch

It sounds fiercely traditional, but this was likely the invention of advertising agents in the 1950s. This one comprises Northern produce.

- Fresh salad greens, dressed
- Hefty slice of Weardale, or other Northern cheese, or
- A slice of Morpeth Terrine (page 91), or pork pie
- Pickled quail eggs
- Stanhope pickle (page 155) or Bishopton Chutney (page 154)
- Slice of crusty bread, such as Newbiggin (page 176)

- Arrange on a plate and accompany with your favourite lunchtime beverage—beer for some, tea for me.

Durham Salad Cream

This makes a great salad dressing and a good dip for raw vegetables.

- Small boiled potatoes - 2
- Durham Mustard - 1 tbs (page 152)
- Vegetable oil - 4 tbs
- Vinegar - 2 tbs
- Egg yolks - 2 hard boiled
- Small onion - 1 mashed to a paste with 1 tsp salt
- Mushroom ketchup or anchovy paste - 1 tsp

- So simple. Purée all the ingredients together in a blender.

Edible Flowers

In the Northern Counties, flowers used to show up in the Summer salads. Whether this was just to add a little extra colour and flavour to the greens, or is perhaps a remnant of older times when flowers had a defined role to play in folk medicine and faerie magic, I don't know. But they certainly cheer up a salad and are an easy way to add colourful interest to a meal. The culinary use of flowers is not new, nor confined to the Northern Counties, of course.

Take care and use only flowers you are certain are edible. If you are not certain, leave them out. Many people suppose that anything on the plate can be eaten, so don't use inedible flowers or flowers from florists, nurseries or garden centres that may have been treated with chemicals. In urban areas, or places where traffic is heavy or confined, roadside flowers grow their entire lives amid clouds of car exhaust. You can taste petroleum fumes in them, and it's not nice. Use only the petals from the flowers—pistils and stamens are often bitter. Remember, too, that at different times of the growing season flowers will have more or less flavour, so what was great in June may be flavourless in July. Don't hide the flowers or cut them so small they can't be picked out. Some people have allergies and they cannot eat certain flowers no matter how pure the source.

Some safe edible flowers of the Northern Counties are borage, calendula (pot marigold) violet, rose, corn flowers, rocket, ramsons (wild garlic), sage, geranium, nasturtium, dandelion, lavender, verbena, dill, rosemary, and chives.

Miner's Salad

Miner's salad is the local name for purslane, a small ground-hugging weed with a slight lemon flavour. It got its name from its popularity with coal miners who would pull up a handful before going underground and chew it to take the taste of coal dust from their mouths.

- Cucumber - 1 large peeled, seeded and cubed
- Medium tomato - 1 chopped
- Purslane - leaves and thinner stems from 1 bunch, chopped
- Fresh squeezed lemon juice - 2 tbs
- Salt - to taste

- Combine all ingredients in a serving bowl. Salt to taste.

Greenhouse Salad

When I was very young, my father and grandfather both had garden allotments on the outskirts of our village. My dad spent many long hours building a large greenhouse out of recycled windowed panels from a local church. The produce from that greenhouse was the most flavourful and fresh. If you are lucky enough to have access to fresh local tomatoes and cucumbers, this is an excellent salad.

- Large tomatoes - 3 cut into wedges
- Large sweet onion - 1 sliced thin
- Large cucumber - 1 sliced
- Vegetable oil - 60ml
- Cider vinegar - 2 tbs
- Garlic - 1 clove minced
- Fresh basil - 1 tsp minced
- Fresh chives - 1 tsp minced
- Salt - $\frac{1}{2}$ tsp

- In a serving bowl, combine tomatoes, onion and cucumber.
- Whisk together the dressing ingredients until blended. Drizzle over salad and serve immediately.

SOUP

~ Beautiful soup! Who cares for fish, game, or any other dish? Who would not give all else for two pennyworth only of beautiful soup? ~ Lewis Caroll - resident of Croft-on-Tees.

One of the best examples of golden food has to be the Autumn soup we had when I was a child. Everything in it came from my father's allotment garden: potatoes, carrots, onions and swedes. Back then it was simmered for hours so that the vegetables melted into a thick, warming broth with a few strokes of a whisk. Today, the velvet consistency can be easily achieved in a blender. Soup is truly a wonderful thing. It's cheap to make, it's easy to make. It tastes better on day two; it can be frozen and kept for much later. It has infinite variation, and it seems to have the capacity to resurrect the past better than most other foods. One whiff of pea and ham and I am transported back several decades to my grandmother's scullery kitchen in County Durham. Pass me a spoon …

How to Make Stock

Many recipes in this book will call for either chicken or beef stock, and you have three options when a recipe calls for this:

- Homemade stock will taste the best, no contest.
- Tinned or tetra-pack stock is a good substitute and very convenient but beware … it's often very high in sodium so go easy on the salt in the rest of the recipe.
- Bullion cubes will do at a pinch.

You'll see onions, celery and carrots listed as the base ingredients for numerous recipes, especially soups, stews and sauces. This basic combination in culinary parlance is sometimes called mirepoix in French and trinity or aromatics in English, and the Northern Counties standard is two parts onion, one part each celery and carrot. If there is a leek available we often add that too.

Stock
- Bare bones - 2 kg cut into 5cm pieces
- Cold water - 4 litres
- Celery stalks - 4 chopped
- Carrots - 6 sliced thick, no need to peel
- Yellow onions - 2 quartered but not peeled (skins adds colour)
- Black peppercorns - 8

- Chicken bones don't need to be roasted, but beef bones should be. Roast the bones uncovered in a 200°C oven for 2 hours (they should be brown, not black).
- Place the bones in a large pot, add vegetables and water.
- Simmer for 2 hours, topping up water as required.
- Strain out all the non-liquid ingredients.
- Place the stock in the refrigerator overnight. Discard the fat that floats to the top and hardens. Chicken stock will gelatinize.

Dumplings

Dumplings, or pot balls, have been popular in the Northern Counties at least since Roman soldiers added them to pottages after a cold day's duty guarding Hadrian's Wall. I suspect dumplings predate written history, from whence the dubious provenance of much food lineage is gleaned.

After I left school at 16, I was an apprentice for half a decade. As I went through that five years I met and worked with some wonderful characters. One such man has an eternal association with dumplings. He used to walk around Aycliffe Trading Estate looking after the drains. He wore a ginger-coloured greatcoat that was tied with a belt. I don't know who employed him, or really what he did, except it was effected with a long metal rod bent to a right-angle at the tip. What was more interesting to me was his 'bait' … that being the vernacular for packed-lunch.

He invariably had a big raw onion, a hefty brick of cheese and a chunk of bread, and he took a bite from each in succession. He also had a stone bottle, these days seen only in museums and TV period dramas, which—he said—contained cold, clear tea. And that's not even the interesting bit … riveting though it is. What was most curious was his lamentation that people no longer had braziers going. Braziers were fires contained in—usually—old oil drums standing on bricks. When they were common it was his custom to have 'pot balls and broth.' He lowered a Billy-can over the hot embers to bring water to a boil into which he dropped a couple of bouillon cubes. Then he added his pot balls: little dumplings made of minced pork and chopped scallions, salt and pepper wrapped in flour-and-water pastry. They were kept in a paper bag with plain flour to keep them from sticking together, and the flour was mixed to a paste with cold water then added to the broth after the dumplings had cooked for 10 minutes and floated to the top. What could be simpler? Apparently these dumplings were once very popular with men who worked out of doors and kept a fire going to keep warm. They were popular too with local land-army girls—those women who helped run the agricultural industry during World War Two when most of the men were away at war. Perhaps their association with those dark days put them out of favour—cheap and simple was the order of the day, but more is the pity because they were also nutritious and tasty.

Pot Balls

Pastry:
- Plain flour - 150g
- Salt - ½ tsp
- Water

- Mix a half-teaspoon of salt with the flour.
- Add water and and mix in gradually until you have a stiff dough. Knead for 10 minutes till smooth and shiny, then let it rest in a covered bowl for an hour.

Filling:
- Minced pork - 100g
- Green onion -1 chopped fine
- Pinch of dried herbs
- Salt & pepper

- Roll the pastry out to about 3mm thick and cut into rounds about 8cm across.
- Place a teaspoon of the mix in the centre, wet the edges and fold over into half-moon shapes.
- Crimp the edges so the dumplings don't leak.

- Boil in broth for about 10 minutes. My favourite broth for these is made by adding a dried kafir lime leaf to a litre of good chicken stock.

Stew Dumplings

These are lovely and warming in the Winter and can be served with all types of soups, stews and casseroles. There are also lots of variations.

- Self-raising flour - 200g
- Salt - ½ tsp
- Shredded suet - 100g
- Mixed herbs – 1 tsp chopped fresh or ½ tsp dried, optional
- Cold water - to mix

- Mix the dry ingredients with water to a soft, elastic dough, roll into balls and add to soups or stews half an hour before serving.

- Herb dumplings: include half an onion, finely grated, and double the amount of herbs.
- Cheese dumplings: add 25g grated cheddar or 1 tbs grated Parmesan cheese.
- Curry dumplings: add ½ tsp mild curry powder.
- Paprika dumplings: add ½ tsp paprika.
- Caraway dumplings: add 1 tsp caraway seeds.

Sippets

Sippets are simply pieces of toasted bread served with soup or stew. Once toasted they are spread with butter and either served immediately or sometimes fried on one side in garlic- or onion-infused fat. They are usually cut into triangles or small rectangles—'soldiers.'

- Slices of bread, toasted, buttered and cut into triangles.

- Fry a clove of garlic, sliced, or ½ a small onion chopped small in a couple of tablespoons of butter or oil, or a combination of both. Discard the garlic/onion and fry the sippets on one side only until crisp. Serve immediately.

Beetroot Soup

Every European country has a recipe for beetroot soup. Indeed, it is so prolific in Russia that the word for soup—borscht—has become synonymous in the English-speaking world for beetroot soup. This recipe comes from one of my mother's notebooks where she calls it 'red soup,' a perfect fit for Northern Counties culinary colours.

- Beetroot - 500g peeled
- Onion - 1 medium, diced
- Potato - 1 medium, peeled
- Vegetable oil - 3 tbs
- Lemon rind - ½ tsp
- Lemon juice - 1 tsp
- Mint leaves - 6 chopped
- Cream - 125ml
- Water - 1.5 litres
- Salt, black pepper to taste

- Peel the beetroots and potato and cut into small pieces.
- Chop lemon rind fine.
- Heat oil in a pan and fry onions for 2 minutes.
- Add to this chopped beetroot, potato and lemon rind.
- Add water and bring to boil for 15 minutes.
- When the vegetables have been boiled, purée them until smooth.
- Add salt, pepper and lemon juice and bring to boil for 10 minutes.
- Garnish with mint leaves and a swirl of cream. Serve hot.

Carrot and Fresh Mint Soup

A soup with a refreshing mint edge. The secret is in adding the fresh mint after the soup is cooked. The original recipe was found, handwritten in beautiful purple ink, in a notebook retrieved from Kendal Library's lost-and-found. It called for mushroom relish and 'large white carrots' so it must be very old— carrots used to be white, but since the 1700s they have been orange.

- Butter - 25g
- Carrots - 700g sliced
- Onion - 1 medium, sliced
- Vegetable stock - 600ml
- Milk - 600ml
- Fresh mint - 2 tbs chopped
- Worcestershire sauce - few drops
- Salt and freshly ground pepper
- Natural yogurt and fresh mint - to garnish

- Melt butter, add carrots and onion and cook for 5 minutes.
- Add stock and milk, cover and simmer gently for 15-20 minutes until vegetables are soft.
- Purée until smooth. Add chopped mint, Worcestershire sauce and seasoning.
- Serve hot or well chilled, garnished with yogurt and fresh mint.

Craster Crab Soup

By! Ha' ye seen the greet big crabs the' catch?
Aal bet ye've nivvor, ivvor seen thor match!
Nee other wonder they sell mony a batch
Fine Craster crabs fresh from the sea!

I went to Craster to get the famous oak-smoked kippers at the recommendation of the late Alan Davison who gave them high praise in his book 'A Kipper for my Tea.' While there I discovered this excellent crab soup in the local pub.

- Crab meat - 225g
- Butter - 50g
- Plain flour - 50g
- Creamy milk - 900ml
- Chicken or fish stock - 1.2 litres
- Salt and white pepper
- Grated nutmeg - $1/4$ tsp
- Double cream - 150ml   *(continued over page)*

- Separate the white and dark crab meat. If you are using cooked crab meat, add it all at the very end just before serving.
- Heat the butter until foaming, stir in the flour and allow to cook for a minute, then add the milk, stirring well, then the chicken or fish stock. Add the dark crab meat, salt, pepper and nutmeg and simmer gently for 12-15 minutes. Add the white crab meat and bring to just under boiling point, simmer for 5 minutes and check for seasoning.
- Transfer to warmed soup bowls, with a swirl of cream in each.

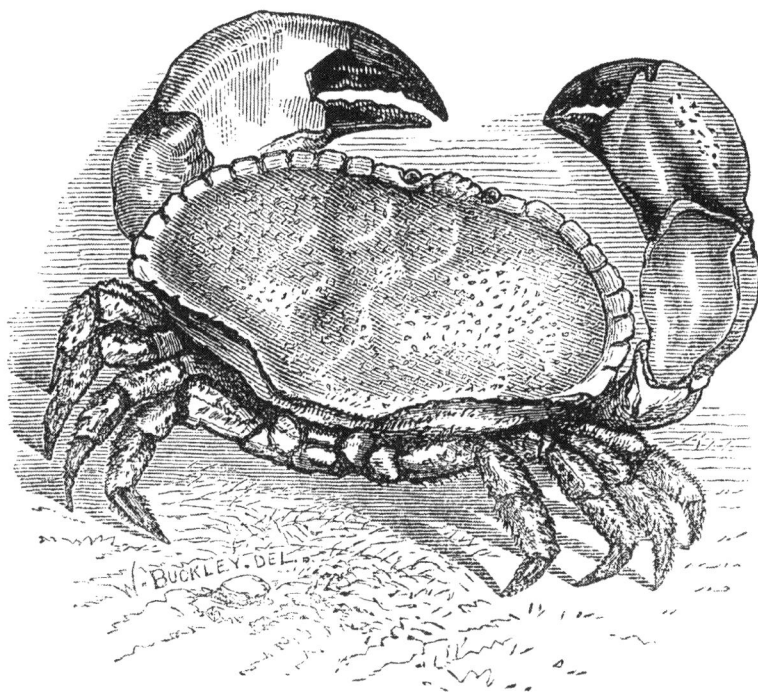

Durham Bacon Broth

This soup is hearty enough to be both first and second courses … a timesaving and delicious meal!

- Shoulder or collar bacon - 900g soaked 8hrs in cold water
- Pearl barley - 2 tbs
- Red lentils - 2 tbs
- Onions - 2 medium, sliced
- Carrots - 4 medium, sliced
- Parsnips - 2 medium, sliced
- Freshly ground black pepper
- Thyme - 1 tsp dried
- Potatoes - 450g sliced
- Cabbage - 1 small, quartered
- Leek - 1 chopped
- Fresh parsley - 1 tbs chopped

- Strain the bacon, then put into a large saucepan with water to cover. Bring to the boil and remove any scum and fats floating on the top.
- Add the pearl barley and the lentils, bring to the boil and simmer for about 25 minutes.
- Add the onions, carrots, parsnips, pepper to taste, and thyme. Return to the boil, lower the heat, cover and simmer gently for half an hour.
- Add the potatoes and cabbage, and simmer until they are tender but not mushy. The barley and the lentils will be soft by this time and the piece of bacon should be cooked through.
- Five minutes before the broth is ready, add the chopped leek and chopped parsley.
- To serve, lift out the bacon and vegetables and serve the broth as the first course. Then chop the bacon into chunks and serve with the vegetables as the second course.

Fish Chowder

A chowder is somewhere between a soup and a stew. In fact, this is more commonly known as fish stew in the Northern Counties. I've eaten a lot of chowder around the world and this is my version. I think it's a winner.

- Thick haddock fillet - 450g skinned
- Onion - 1 small, chopped fine
- Milk - 850ml
- Fish stock - 300ml
- Potatoes - 3, peeled and cubed
- Mushrooms, 4 sliced
- Bacon rashers - 110g rinded and diced
- Salt and freshly ground pepper
- Evaporated milk – 250ml

- Cut the haddock into small pieces.
- In a large saucepan, fry the onion with the bacon in a little oil until the onions are translucent and the bacon has given up its fat, then add the milk and stock and bring slowly to the boil.
- When the milk and water come to the boil, add the potatoes and mushrooms, season with a little salt and pepper and simmer, covered, for half an hour.
- Add the haddock and cook for a further 10 minutes, taste for seasoning, stir in the evaporated milk and serve at once.

Northumbrian Cockle Soup

They say that originally the cockles for this soup were boiled in sea water. I hope they didn't use it as stock ... salt water makes you mad.

- Cockles - 40-50
- Butter - 25g
- Plain flour - 25g
- Milk - 600ml
- Onion - 2 tbs chopped fine
- Celery - 2 tbs chopped fine
- Parsley - 2 tbs chopped plus extra for garnish
- Cream - 4-6 tbs

- Scrub the cockle shells well under cold running water, discarding any that are already open.
- Place the cockles in a large saucepan and cover with cold, well-salted water.
- Bring slowly to the boil, shake the saucepan from time to time. As soon as the cockles open they are ready—over-cooking will make them tough.
- Strain, reserving the stock, then quickly put the cockles into cold water to cool.
- When cool, discard the water and remove the cockles from their shells using a sharp knife.
- Strain the cooled stock again and make up to 900ml with water if necessary.
- Melt the butter in a saucepan.
- Add the onion and celery and cook, stirring, for 5-10 minutes, or until the vegetables are soft.
- Stir in the flour and cook for 1 minute.
- Gradually add the cockle stock, stirring to prevent lumps forming. Bring to the boil then stir in the milk.
- Add the parsley and season to taste, then stir in the cockles.
- Heat through thoroughly and pour into 4-6 soup bowls. Swirl a tablespoon of cream into each bowl and garnish with a little parsley. Serve with crusty bread.

Grouse and Lentil Soup

Growing up in County Durham, the only times I ever saw grouse was either when they burst out of the heather up on the moors and scared the life out of me, or in the late Summer as they hung in butchers' shops in Darlington. Even then my interest was in trying to pluck a feather to make fishing flies without getting caught. The first time I tasted grouse was in this soup.

- Vegetable oil - 2 tbs
- Carrots - 3 peeled and diced
- Onions - 2 peeled and diced
- Lentils - 100g
- Celery - 3 stalks sliced thin

(continued over page)

- Small white turnip or parsnip peeled and diced
- Grouse meat - 1kg cut into cubes
- Chicken broth - 1 litre
- Parsley, rosemary, allspice, salt and pepper

- Put about 2 tbs of oil into a soup pot, add three diced carrots, 2 onions cut up, three stalks of celery sliced and the turnip or parsnip. Cook this with a cover for about 15 minutes, stir occasionally.
- Add the chicken broth and the lentils. Put in the grouse cut into cubes, add some parsley, a little rosemary, allspice, salt and pepper.
- Simmer all of this for an hour and a half. Just before serving you may add a splash of dry sherry and a little more parsley.

Leek and Potato Soup

If the Northern Counties were an independent state, leek and potato would be the national soup.

- Leeks - 2
- Potato - 1 medium
- Butter - 25g
- Bay leaf - 1
- Water - 900ml
- Single cream - 150ml
- Parsley - 1-2 tbs, chopped

- Wash and chop the leeks, discarding the really tough green leaves, but using as much of the green part as possible. Peel and chop the potato.
- Cook these very gently in the butter together with the bay leaf for about 10 minutes, stirring occasionally, but do not let them brown.
- Add the water and simmer gently for about 30 minutes, then push through a sieve or liquidize.
- Return to the pan, add the cream, parsley and season to taste. Serve immediately.

Pea and Ham Soup

You may recognize these soups as pease pudding thinned with good stock. You'd be correct. Confusingly, there are two types of pea and ham soup commonly served in the Northern Counties. One is green and the other gold. If you wanted to be truly adventurous with our culinary colours, you could make another with red lentils and compete a tricolour flag! Serve with some crusty Batten Bread (page 177) for a hearty Winter dish.

Green Pea and Ham

- Split green peas - 450g
- Onions - 2 chopped fine
- Ham bone - 800g
- Freshly ground pepper
- Bay leaf - 1
- Butter - 15g
- Chicken stock - 1 litre

- Soak the peas overnight. The following day, strain the peas and place them in a large saucepan with the ham, pepper and bay leaf and cover with stock. Simmer gently for 2 hours, covered.
- Remove the ham bone and when cool, pick off all the meat and return it to the soup. Check the seasoning and adjust if necessary.

Gold Pea and Ham - use yellow lentils in place of green peas.

Red Lentil - simply use the above recipe and substitute red lentils.

Creamy Potato Soup

Potatoes are as much a staple in the Northern Counties as they are in Ireland. Immigrants from Ulster brought this simple recipe in the mid-1800s and it remains a favourite today.

- Potatoes - 450g diced
- Onion - 1 large sliced thin
- Celery - 2 medium sticks, sliced
- Butter - 25g

(continued over page)

- Water - 450ml
- Salt and freshly ground pepper
- Milk - 300ml
- Cream - 3 tbs (optional)
- Fresh parsley or chives - 2 tbs, chopped

- In a saucepan fry vegetables gently in butter for 10 minutes without browning. Add water and season to taste. Bring to the boil, cover and simmer gently for 25 minutes.
- Liquidize or rub through a sieve, return to the pan and stir in milk. Bring to the boil, stirring and simmer for 5 minutes.
- Ladle into warm soup bowls. Whirl on fresh cream if used and sprinkle with parsley.

Ramson Soup

This verdant Spring soup may be enriched with cream, in which case the colour will be more pastel. To keep the flavour bright, be sure to add the garlic leaves after cooking the potato in the stock. This soup is good hot or cold.

- Unsalted butter - 2 tbs
- Medium onion - 1 peeled and chopped fine
- Potatoes - 450g peeled and cut into 1cm pieces
- Vegetable stock - 500ml
- Wild garlic leaves - 3 generous handfuls
- Coarse salt and freshly ground pepper to taste

- In a heavy-bottomed saucepan, gently fry the onion in the butter until softened but not coloured.
- Add the vegetable stock and potatoes and bring to the boil.
- Simmer for 15-20 minutes, until the potatoes are cooked.
- Blend the soup in a food processor.
- Now add the raw garlic leaves and blend again until the leaves have melded into the soup.
- Season with salt and pepper to taste.

Six Onion Soup

My dad claimed he invented this soup after a bumper year for the allium family on his allotment.

- Unsalted butter - 125g
- Yellow onions - 2 diced
- Large leeks - 4 cleaned and sliced thin, using white and light green parts only
- Shallots - 4 chopped
- Scallions - 4 chopped
- Garlic cloves - 6 peeled and chopped
- Dry cider - 250ml
- Chicken stock - 1 litre
- Fresh thyme - 1 sprig
- Bay leaf - 1
- Salt and pepper to taste
- Double cream - 250ml
- Fresh chives - 1 bunch chopped fine or cut with scissors

- Melt the butter in a large soup pot over high heat.
- Add the onions, leeks, scallions and shallots and cook on medium-low heat until the ingredients are tender but not browned. Add the garlic last and sweat 5 minutes further.
- Add the dry cider and stir to remove any browned bits from the bottom of the pot. Add the stock, thyme, bay leaf, salt, and pepper.
- Partially cover and simmer and for 20 minutes. Purée ingredients and return the soup to the pot.
- Bring the soup back to a simmer and add the cream. Ladle soup into warm bowls and sprinkle with fresh chives to garnish.

Sorrel Soup

Sorrel is available from supermarkets but it also grows wild in Northern England. It's a robust plant with sharply pointed leaves and red flowers and has an almost lemony taste. As kids, we would chew on sorrel, which we called sour dock, or soury ducks, when we got thirsty wandering the fields. Ideally, it should be picked in the Spring when it is young and fresh.

- Sorrel leaves - 2 handfuls chopped fine
- Butter - 50g
- Light stock - 1.5 litres
- Egg yolks - 2
- Salt and pepper

- Melt the butter in a pan and stew the sorrel gently over a low heat for 5 minutes. Do not allow the butter to brown.
- Add the stock and bring to the boil, clearing any scum from the surface. Season.
- Beat the egg yolks thoroughly in a serving bowl then pour the boiling soup over them, whisking with a fork.
- Serve immediately with hot crusty bread and a bland cheese.

Roasted Tomato Soup

Unbelievably superior to the tinned stuff.

- Fresh tomatoes - 1kg washed, cored and halved
- Garlic - 6 cloves peeled and chopped
- Small yellow onions - 2 sliced
- Vegetable oil - 100ml
- Salt and freshly ground black pepper
- Chicken stock - 1 litre
- Bay leaves - 2
- Butter - 4 tbs
- Fresh basil leaves - small bunch chopped (optional)
- Cream - 175ml (optional)

Preheat oven to 230°C

- Spread the tomatoes, garlic cloves and onions onto a baking tray. Drizzle with oil and season with salt and pepper. Roast for 20 to 30 minutes.
- Remove roasted tomatoes, garlic and onion from the oven and transfer to a large stock pot. Add ¾ of the chicken stock, bay leaves, and butter. Bring to a boil, reduce heat and simmer for 15 to 20 minutes or until liquid has reduced by a third.
- Wash and dry basil leaves, if using, and add to the pot. Use an immersion blender to purée the soup until smooth. Return soup to low heat, add cream and adjust consistency with remaining chicken stock, if necessary. Season to taste with salt and freshly ground black pepper. Serve with a swirl of cream.

Me Da's Leek Broth

We used to beg my dad not to put the cabbage in, but he always did. Nowadays I won't have it any other way. I suspect this dish came with the Welsh in the mid-1800s, as it's almost identical to Cawl Cennin, the national soup of Wales. I stand to be corrected, as usual.

- Large leek - 1
- Small white cabbage - 1
- Swede turnip - ½ medium
- Carrots - 2 large
- Parsnips - 1 medium
- Potatoes - 2 large

- Cut everything into small cubes then place in a large saucepan and cover with water. Boil ingredients until they're as tender as you like them.
- Seasoning: Swede turnips (or snaggers—or narkies if you're from Haswell way) are pretty peppery so you might want to cook this a while before adding more seasoning. I think the experts have agreed salt is not so bad for you as once believed so fill yer boots. I always cheat and add a couple of chicken bullion cubes anyway.

- If it cooks a long time the taties will drop apart and the broth will thicken. Some like it thin, mind. Or you could thicken it by adding cornflour and water to the boil. Or—if tradition allows— you can purée a couple of ladlefuls of the veggies in a blender and add them back to the soup.

Mushroom and Leek Soup

If you don't have mushroom ketchup, use Worcestershire sauce or, better still, Yorkshire Relish, which will give the soup what is in many parts of the Northern Counties called 'a little snap.'

- Butter - 25g
- Leeks - 2 sliced
- Mushrooms - 225g sliced
- Milk - 600ml
- Chicken or vegetable stock - 300ml
- Mushroom ketchup - 1 tbs
- Ground bay leaves - pinch
- Cornflour - 3 tbs
- Sherry - 3 tbs
- Freshly ground pepper - a pinch
- Chives - chopped, to garnish

- Melt the butter in a large pan, add the sliced leeks and mushrooms and cook for 5 minutes or until soft.
- Add milk, stock, mushroom ketchup and ground bay leaves and bring to the boil and simmer for 20 minutes.
- Blend the cornflour with the sherry and stir into soup and cook for 2 minutes.
- Garnish with chopped chives to serve.

VEGETABLES

It would be a sorry day if cooks lost all sense of the seasons. Even though we can obtain Spring and Summer produce all year round there is real pleasure in serving fresh vegetables. Old cookery books from the Northern Counties tend not to have many recipes for individual vegetable preparation. Most were cooked in with either soups or stews, or are so simplistic and common to not warrant a recipe as such. There are some interesting exceptions of course.

Leeks

Scarred coal miners wearing pretty little flowers in their lapels seems odd. But I suppose if you toiled in the blackness of a pit you'd be partial to those jewels of the sunlight. Birds—primarily pigeons—were also a popular hobby among those that worked the mines. Canaries and finches used to be kept in almost every house in a mining village at one time. Miners loved all growing things. The fashion has changed, and men no longer wear a 'buttonhole,' but the tradition continues through the hundreds of flower and vegetable shows at the end of Summer all over the North. Leeks, especially, have achieved something of cult status among those who grow them.

Most of the world knows this humble plant as a tall skinny onion or a really big scallion. In most of the world a big 'un might be as thick as your wrist, but in the North East they can grow them as thick as a man's leg. This is not the culinary leek—although it is perfectly edible—but the leek of mythology that grows in secret and guarded environs away from the scrutiny of rivals and scurrilous saboteurs.

OK, what to do with all them leeks ... well, in many places tradition has it that they go into a leek soup and get dished out to all and sundry in the pub the evening of the leek show. The other default dish is leek pudding.

Leek Pudding

I've never owned a pan big enough to hold a roly-poly leek pudding so mine's made in a deep flat pan. If you want the traditional shape, simply roll the suet pastry in an oblong, cover with the leeks and roll it up, then wrap it in a floured tea towel. Tie the tea towel at the ends and drop it into a BIG pan of boiling water for an hour-and-a-half. Running cold water over the pudding for one minute just after you take it from the boiling water will stop it becoming gluey (or 'claggy' as they say in the Northern Counties). Otherwise follow this recipe for a traditional bowl-shaped pudding. Either shape is excellent served with lashings of gravy. You can substitute chilled and grated shortening, butter, margarine, lard etc. for the suet. You can now even get vegetarian suet but all these will lack the authentic suet flavour (I can live without it). A few dried herbs helps the dough too.

- Suet pastry - 500g (page 120)
- Cold water
- Leeks - 500g

- Clean and chop the leeks.
- Prepare a pie dish about 10cm deep suitable for steaming (glass, pyrex, tin whatever you've got), lightly grease inside with oil or margarine.
- Bring a large pan of water to the boil.
- Cut pastry into two pieces — ⅔ and ⅓. Roll out ⅔ to line your dish, put leeks into lined dish then roll out ⅓ to make a lid.
- Cover top of pie dish with sheet of greaseproof paper and secure it in place (a bit string or a rubber band comes in handy here)
- Gently lower dish into the pan (water should only reach ⅔ up the height of your dish and should not make contact with the pudding. Refill during cooking—never let it dry out.
- Boil the pudding for one and a half hours. Serve.

Sage Roasted Potatoes

Don't feel restricted to sage—other herbs go really well with potatoes.

- Potatoes - 1.5kg
- Vegetable oil - 45ml
- Dried sage - 1 tsp
- Garlic paste - 1 tsp
- Salt - ¾ tsp
- Ground black pepper - 1 tsp

- Peel and cube potatoes. Parboil in boiling salted water for 5 minutes. This will give you fluffy edges that go crisp during baking. Drain and let cool slightly then toss with oil and garlic paste, sprinkle with salt, pepper and dried sage.

- Spread on large baking sheet and roast in 160°C oven for 1 hour. Increase heat to 230°C and roast, turning once, until tender, crispy and golden, about 25 minutes.

Pan Haggerty (pronounced pa-NAKEL-tee)

An inexpensive, warming and welcome dish from Northumberland and Durham. There are many variations on this basic potato and onion theme, this one with cheese, others with mushrooms or minced beef—use your imagination. Adding a lamb chop per person just beneath the last layer of potatoes turns this homely dish into 'Panjotheram.'

• Butter - 25g
• Vegetable oil - 1 tbs
• Potatoes - 450g peeled and sliced thin
• Onions - 2 medium, sliced thin
• Cheddar or Lancashire cheese - 110g grated

- Heat the butter and oil in a large heavy-based or non-stick frying pan. Remove the pan from the heat and put in layers of potatoes, onions and grated cheese ending with a top layer of cheese.
- Cover and cook gently for 30 minutes or until the veg is cooked.
- Remove the lid and brown the top of the Pan Haggerty under a hot grill. Serve straight from the pan.

Cousin Jim

This variation on Pan Haggerty shows how families utilized whatever was on hand. It comes from Binchester and was made for 'Tuesday dinner' there and in surrounding villages. Simple, nourishing and delicious comfort food.

"Slice some onions and place them in the bottom of a dripping pan and lay on top of them slices of liver and bacon. Then put the dripping tin in a moderate oven and cook until everything is nicely done."

Carlin Pea Cakes

"Tid, Mid, Miseray, Carlin, Palm, Pace-Egg Day" Carlins, or carlings, or pigeon peas, were served during lent and until recently showed up all over the Northern Counties, and especially on Tyneside, on Carlin Sunday on pub bars as a snack. In pubs they were normally seen just boiled then quickly pickled in vinegar or sometimes soaked in rum. In years past they were made into these little cakes and fried.

- Carlin peas - 200g
- Fresh white breadcrumbs - 60g
- Onion - 1 peeled and chopped fine
- Parsley - 1 tbs chopped fine
- Salt - pinch
- Black pepper - pinch
- Butter - 1 tbs melted
- Butter - 1 tbs for frying

- Soak the peas overnight in cold water. Drain and rinse well.
- Place in a saucepan and cover in fresh cold water*. Bring to boil and simmer for about 1 hour or more until tender. Drain.
- When cool, mix with breadcrumbs, onion, parsley salt, pepper and the melted butter to form a stiff mixture.
- Shape into cakes and fry gently in butter to crisp, golden brown. Serve hot.

* Do NOT salt the water, as this toughens the skins and prevents the inside of the peas from rehydrating during cooking.

Cumbrian Cabbage

In my opinion, this recipe from Appleby-in-Westmoreland makes the best cabbage. Still crunchy and with lots of flavour it makes an elegant side dish for those high-days when only the best will do.

- White cabbage - 1 small
- Butter - 1 tbs
- Chicken stock - 4 tbs
- Sugar - 1 tbs

(continued over page)

- Fresh nutmeg - a grating to taste
- Black pepper - pinch
- Fresh parsley - 2tbs
- Salt - to taste
- Lemon juice - 1 tbs

- Wash the cabbage, remove the core and slice into 3cm wedges.
- Combine the butter and stock in a large pan, add the cabbage sprinkled with sugar, nutmeg and black pepper.
- Cover pan and cook over high heat until it begins to steam, then reduce heat and simmer gently until just cooked through, about 15 minutes.
- Toss with more butter, then transfer to serving dish and sprinkle with fresh parsley, salt and lemon juice. Serve immediately.

Braised Red Cabbage

Brassicas grow well in the North. Red cabbage is a favourite because of both taste and colour. Braised red cabbage makes a great accompaniment to roast pork, duck, rabbit and other game dishes.

- Red cabbage - 1kg
- Onions - 2 chopped
- Cooking apples - 2,peeled, cored and coarse-grated
- Grated nutmeg - 1 tsp
- Ground cloves - $1/4$ tsp
- Ground cinnamon - $1/4$ tsp
- Fresh thyme - $1/4$ tsp
- Soft brown sugar - 1 tbs
- Red wine vinegar - 3 tbs
- Butter - 25g

Pre-heat oven to 170°C.

- Cut off and discard the large white ribs from the outer leaves of the cabbages then shred it fine.
- Layer the shredded cabbage in a large ovenproof dish with the onions, apples, nutmeg, cloves, cinnamon, thyme and sugar.

Pour the wine vinegar over it. Cut the butter into cubes and scatter over the mixture.

- Cover the dish and cook in the oven for about 1½ hours, stirring a couple of times, until the cabbage is very tender. Serve hot.

Roasted Cauliflower

My dad could grow magnificent cauliflowers in his allotment garden, and I always felt a bit guilty that I didn't like them much. I didn't get a taste for cauliflower until I was an adult, but cooked elegantly like this, it doesn't need to be smothered in cheese sauce for your kids to eat it.

- Large cauliflower - 1 cut into florets
- Vegetable oil - 4 tsp
- Garlic - 3 cloves peeled and pressed
- Salt - ½ tsp
- Sugar - ¼ tsp
- Fresh rosemary - 2 tsp chopped fine
- Ground black pepper - ¼ tsp
- Cider vinegar - ½ tsp

- Place everything in a large bowl and and toss until well coated. Marinate for at least an hour and up to 24 hours in the fridge.
- Spread the cauliflower onto a large baking sheet and bake for about 15 minutes in a 250°C oven.
- Turn the pieces of cauliflower and bake for another 10-15 minutes, until lightly browned and tender.

Onions

I remember once watching a TV news program, which featured the 'very last onion seller'—a Frenchman, suitably attired in blue-hooped shirt and black beret. He had travelled each year with his father to South Shields where they warehoused the onions. From there they set out on bicycles, adorned with the traditional garland of braided

onions, to sell their wares door-to-door and face-to-face to the canny housewives of Tyneside. It was odd to hear a Frenchman speak with a Geordie accent, but they had learned their English first-hand from their customers as they bartered and bargained back and forth in the vernacular of keelmen, fisherfolk and colliers.

Pop-ally Onions

Pop-allys was the name we gave marbles, whether they were made of glass, marble or anything else. The name derived from olden times when the first fizzy drinks bottles were stoppered by a combination of pressure and a little ball made of alabaster. Kids would smash the pop bottles to get the ball from the pop bottle … hence pop-allys.

- Small white onions - 450g peeled
- Butter - 4 tbs
- Chicken stock - 4 tbs
- Sugar - 1 tbs
- Salt - pinch

- Place the onions in a small saucepan, cover in cold water and bring to the boil. Remove immediately and drain.
- Put them back in the saucepan and add the butter and stock, sugar and salt.
- Simmer over low heat until the stock is absorbed and the onions are tender and have just begun to colour.

Whitley Goose

Like so many English dishes, this one is not what the name suggests—there is no goose in it. A homely but rich dish from the Northumberland seaside town.

- Onions - 4 peeled but left whole
- Cheddar cheese - 125g grated
- Single cream - 350ml
- Salt and black pepper
- Butter - a knob

- Boil the onions in lightly salted water until tender (15–20 mins)

- Drain and allow to cool a little.
- Chop onions roughly and mix with half the cheese in a buttered ovenproof dish.
- Pour in the cream then top with the remaining cheese.
- Bake in preheated oven at 200°C for 20-30 minutes or until golden brown.

Turmit n' Tatie

This is how I first ate swedes from the allotment, which, I'm afraid, I did not appreciate when I was a nipper. When mixed with potato, however, I found them delicious, especially as a topping for Shepherd's Pie.

- Potatoes - 500g
- Swede - 500g
- Onion - 1 chopped fine
- Chives - 1 tbs chopped
- Butter and milk
- Salt and pepper

- Peel the potatoes and swede. Cube both but make potatoes roughly half the size of swede so they reach tenderness at the same time. Put into a deep pan with the onions. Add boiling water to cover and simmer gently until the ingredients are just soft. Drain off the cooking liquor.
- Mash everything thoroughly, adding chives and enough milk and butter to make a light consistency. Season with salt and pepper and serve as you would plain mashed potato.

Fried Brussels Sprouts

It was and remains difficult to convince some people that Brussels sprouts are delicious. This recipe will convert many diehard haters.

- Brussels sprouts – 1k trimmed and cut in half lengthwise
- Oil for deep frying
- Coarse salt - to taste

(continued over page)

dressing:
- Garlic clove – 1 skinned, crushed and chopped fine
- Sea salt – ¼ tsp
- Ground cayenne pepper - pinch
- Lime juice - 1½ tbs
- Vegetable oil - 1 tbs

- Place garlic, salt, cayenne, lime juice and vegetable oil in a bowl. Whisk until well blended and set aside.
- Heat a deep-fat fryer to 190°C. Place the sprouts in a wire basket and lower them into the oil. Cover the pan to prevent splattering.
- Fry the sprouts for 5-6 minutes, until golden-brown. Drain on paper towels.
- Place the sprouts in a large bowl and drizzle with the garlic-lime dressing and toss until well coated.
- Sprinkle with sea salt and serve immediately.

Christmas Brussels Sprouts

I don't know why I call them this, as it's the same recipe I use almost every time I serve Brussels sprouts. There are never any leftovers.

- Brussels sprouts - 1kg trimmed, cut in half, including loose leaves
- Streaky bacon - 500g chopped into small pieces
- Chicken stock - 250ml

- Cook bacon in a frying pan until crisp and the fat is rendered.
- Remove the bacon pieces but leave all the fat in the pan.
- Add sprouts and cook on high heat until they take a little colour
- Add stock and bacon pieces and cover with a lid.
- Lower the heat and cook for 10 minutes. The sprouts should still have a bit of snap left to them.
- Once the stock has all gone add a lump of butter.

Durham Parsnips

I serve these at every special occasion and they are always well received.

- Parsnips - 500g peeled and shaved, or diced
- Butter - 1 tbs
- Durham Mustard - 2 tbs (page 152)

- Fry the parsnips in the butter on low heat until tender.
- Add the mustard and stir until well coated.

Fried Leeks

A recipe from 1890. It sensibly recommends eating the leeks with the bacon and a thick-cut slice of crusty bread accompanied by a mug of tea.

- Bacon fat - whatever is rendered from previously cooked good bacon
- Leeks - 2 medium sized cut into 25mm lengths, both green and white parts
- Hot water - 4 tbs

- After frying good quality bacon, remove from the pan and add chopped leeks and the hot water.
- Cover and cook gently until tender. Keep an eye on the water and never let it go dry—the gravy is delicious.

MUSHROOMS

OK, mushrooms are not vegetables, but in cookery we treat them as such. According to Peggy Hutchinson in her book *Farmhouse Recipes*, the Northern Counties housewife "makes fullest use of the mushroom." And so she should.

I can still remember the first time I found a wild mushroom. It was *Agaricus campestris*, the meadow mushroom, although at the time I only knew it was a mushroom. There were two of them that appeared as if by magic at my feet during a foray into a pasture between the villages of Witton Park and Toft Hill. As I gazed mesmerized at the bright, white caps in the cool grass of late Summer, my friend bent down and picked them both before I realized what was happening. We found no more that day and I never did get to taste one. But I never forgot the thrill of discovery and have sought out wild fungus ever since. Chanterelles by the bucketful, boletes, russulas, puffballs and angel wings. But even if you can't find wild ones, the shops are full of interesting cultivated varieties such as oyster, portobello, shiitake and the ubiquitous but good button mushroom.

NOTE: Many people are wary of wild fungus. Rightly so, for eating the poisonous varieties can cause extreme illness and even death. Make sure you know what you're eating, and if you are not certain, don't eat it.

North Country Mushrooms

Today, country knowledge has been largely lost along with much rural lore and now hardly anyone collects wild mushrooms. Button or chestnut mushrooms can be used in this recipe if the wild ones aren't available.

- Butter - 25g
- Mushrooms (preferably wild ones) - 450g
- Plain flour - 1 tbs
- Milk - 150ml
- Durham Mustard - 2 tsp (page 152)
- Tarragon - 1 tsp chopped
- Soured cream - 3 tbs
- Salad leaves - to serve

- Melt the butter in a pan and cook the mushrooms for a minute or two. Stir in the flour then slowly add the milk. Heat, stirring continuously until thickened. Simmer for 2 minutes.
- Stir in the mustard, chopped tarragon and soured cream.
- Serve on a nest of chicory and lettuce leaves and garnish with tarragon leaves.

Chanterelle Skirlie

Skirlie is a simple toasted-oat dish more common in Scotland than England, but it has its aficionados in Cumbria where it usually contains mushrooms.

- Chanterelles (or any wild mushroom) - 250g diced
- Meat dripping - 150ml
- Onions - 2 diced
- Medium oatmeal - 450g
- Salt and black pepper

- Fry mushrooms in a tablespoon of dripping. Remove and reserve.
- Fry the onion in the remainder of the dripping. When soft but not brown, increase the heat.
- Add the oatmeal, turn it in the dripping for about 5 minutes until it becomes browned slightly. Add the mushrooms, and salt and black pepper to taste. Serve hot.

Mushrooms with Durham Mustard

- Flat mushrooms - 4 very large or 8 medium
- Vegetable oil - 2 tbs
- Garlic - 2 cloves peeled and crushed
- Natural yogurt - 3 tbs
- Durham Mustard - 2 tbs (page 152)
- Bread - 4 thick slices toasted
- Freshly ground black pepper

- In a small bowl, mix the oil with the garlic, brush over the mushrooms, season and grill for 3-4 minutes. Turn each over and brush with the remaining oil and grill for a further 2-3 minutes until cooked.
- To serve, place 1 or 2 mushrooms on top of each slice of hot toasted bread. Mix together the yogurt and mustard, drizzle over the mushrooms and serve at once.

PULSES

Butter Barley

This dish is the Northern Counties' answer to risotto. It utilizes barley, the common cereal crop of the area. It's a welcoming, homely side dish of the highest standard.

- Pearl barley - 125g
- Safflower oil - 1 tsp
- Carrots - 3 tbs shredded fine
- Onions - 3 tbs minced
- Celery - 3 tbs minced
- Fresh rosemary leaves - 1 sprig stripped and chopped fine
- Lovage - 1 tbs chopped fine
- Chicken stock - 375 - 500ml
- Salt - 1 tsp (or less, depending on saltiness of stock)
- Ground black pepper - to taste
- Butter - 2 tbs
- Chopped parsley - a handful

- Put barley in a heavy pan over low heat and toast to light-brown colour. Shake pan frequently to be sure it doesn't get too dark.
- Remove from heat and set aside in a bowl.
- Heat oil in pan, add minced vegetables and sweat for 3 minutes. Add barley and stir to coat grains.
- Add rosemary and stock.
- Simmer, covered, until barley is tender and liquid is absorbed, about 35 minutes.
- Remove from heat and let sit for 5 minutes.
- Fluff with fork. Stir in butter and parsley.

Pease Pudding

Pease pudding is nowadays often met as a sandwich filler and is an old favourite with sliced roast pork or sliced boiled ham. It was once a food seen too often in times of poverty as suggested in the famous nursery rhyme:

Pease pudding hot, Pease pudding cold,
Pease pudding in the pot, Nine days old.

- Dried yellow peas - 250g soaked overnight and drained, or yellow lentils - 250g (don't need soaking)
- Onion - 1 sliced fine
- Fresh rosemary - 1 sprig
- Hambone - 1
- Water - 300ml
- Egg - 1 beaten
- Butter - 15g
- Ground white pepper - ¼ tsp

- Put the first four ingredients into a large saucepan with a lid and cook over gentle heat until the peas start to split. It should take about an hour.
- Check during the simmering and add boiling water if necessary.
- Drain peas and remove the hambone and the rosemary.
- Add remaining ingredients and blend until smooth. The heat from the peas will cook the egg and the pudding will set as it cools.

Brancepeth Baked Beans

Who doesn't love baked beans? Served as part of hearty breakfast or more simply on toast, they are an excellent source of fibre and are inexpensive. You can cheat on this recipe if you must. Instead of starting from scratch with dried beans, use tinned small white beans. Everything else, however, must be done if you want the real thing.

- Dried beans - 1kg
- Cold water - 5 litres
- Onions - 4 medium diced

(continued over page)

- Smoked bacon - 4 rashers sliced fine
- Garlic - 2 cloves minced
- Golden syrup - 500ml
- Treacle - 175ml
- Tomato sauce or chopped tomato, or juice - 250ml
- Dried ginger - 1 tbs or 2 tbs grated fresh ginger
- Durham Mustard - 1 tbs (page 152)
- Salt - 2 tsp salt
- Black pepper - 1 tsp
- Malt vinegar - 2 tbs

- Rinse beans, cover in water and soak overnight. Drain beans (discard soaking water) and combine them in large saucepan with 5 litres of fresh, cold water. Simmer until almost tender, about 45 minutes. Drain, reserving cooking liquid.
- Heat bacon (you'll need a large ovenproof casserole dish, or a bean pot) over medium heat on stovetop to render the bacon fat. When the bacon begins to get crisp, add the beans, onions and garlic and stir for 5 minutes.
- Stir in the treacle, golden syrup, ginger, dry mustard, salt, pepper, and tomato juice. Add enough of the reserved cooking liquid to just cover the beans.
- Cover and bake in 175°C oven for about 3 hours, or until beans are tender. Check throughout cooking, adding more of the reserved cooking liquid if beans begin to dry out.
- Stir vinegar into beans when they are tender and serve.

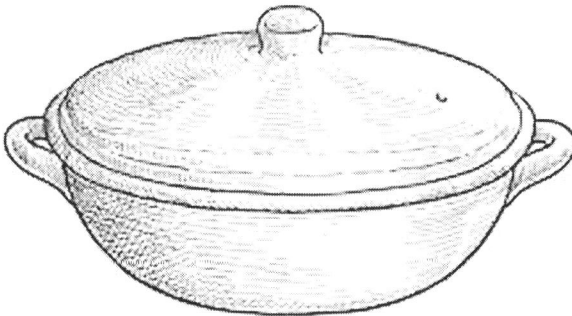

FISH

Many of the Northern Counties' rivers, the Tweed the celebrated exception, lost their salmon and sea-trout runs due to pollution and overfishing. Char, once a sea-running fish lake-locked by the retreating ice sheet at the end of the last great ice-age, have been dramatically reduced in numbers from the Lake District. Burbot, once abundant in the rivers of the North Riding, have, alas, almost certainly been extirpated. The good news is that we seem to have finally come to or senses and cleaner waters have allowed the return of these beautiful fresh water residents and migrants.

Sea Trout with Butter Barley — Serves 4

I caught my first (and only) sea trout under the viaduct over the River Wear at Witton Park a long time ago. Although large, it had already spawned and was in terrible condition, so I released it back into the river to meet a more natural end than it would have got had it been pristine. Since then I have used farmed trout for this dish with great success. It's a very buttery fish that is well-complemented by the Butter Barley.

- Sea trout fillets - 4 pin-boned
- Salt and freshly ground black pepper
- Vegetable oil - 4 tbs
- Lemon juice - 1 tsp

- Season the sea trout fillets.
- Add a splash of oil to a non-stick frying pan and cook the fillets skin-side down for about 5 minutes.
- Turn them over and cook for a further 3-4 minutes.
- Remove from the frying pan and serve on top of Butter Barley (page 38).

Poached Salmon — Serves 2

They say if you can boil water you can poach salmon, and really that's all there is to this dish. The servings here are for two, perfect for a romantic dinner. Many people who don't normally care for fish will eat fresh salmon because it is meaty and never has that fishy taste.

- Salmon fillets, 2 large, skin on, pin-boned
- Water - 1 litre
- Salt - 2tsp
- White wine vinegar - 2tbs
- Parsley to garnish
- Hollandaise sauce (optional)

- Add the water to a wide, shallow frying pan or saucepan that's just large enough to hold the salmon fillets and bring to the boil.

- Add the salt and vinegar.
- Reduce heat to gentle simmer and carefully add the salmon, skin side down. Poach 7-8 minutes.
- Remove the frying pan from the heat and allow the fish to rest for 2 minutes.
- Serve with a hollandaise sauce and warm potato salad or Butter Barley (page 38)

Tweed Kettle

A slightly more sophisticated version of poached salmon, but just as easy to prepare. The Tweed is one of the world's most famous salmon rivers and by tradition the first salmon of the season is presented to the Duke of Northumberland.

- Salmon - 1.5kg
- Shallots - 2 chopped
- Salt and fresh ground pepper
- Stock - 250ml (use the poaching water)
- White wine - 250ml
- Ground mace - pinch
- Parsley - 2 tbs chopped

- Put salmon in a kettle (large saucepan) and cover with water.
- Bring to boil, simmer 5 minutes only.
- Remove from water and reserve a cupful as stock.
- Remove skin and bones from salmon. Cut into cubes.
- Season with salt, pepper, mace.
- Return to saucepan with reserved stock water, wine and shallots.
- Cover, simmer very slowly for about 25 minutes.
- Remove salmon with a slotted spoon, sprinkle it with chopped parsley and serve with either mashed potatoes or Turmit n' Tatie (page 33).

Woof n' Chips—Serves 4

Woof is the northern name for the Wolf fish (Anarhichas lupus), but in Whitby and Scarborough I have heard it also called a catfish. Just to add further confusion, in North Shields the monkfish is known as a catfish ... where they also call a small haddock a chat, and what I call a huss is known there as a Sweet William. You can start a fight by suggesting you have the best recipe for fish and chips. There are so many regional variations, so many family versions and individual nuances that the permutations for getting the best results are endless. Thankfully, this one works very well with any firm-fleshed white fish.

Chips:
- Starchy potatoes - 4
- Dripping or oil, for frying

- Peel and cut potatoes into uniform chips.
- Heat the fat in a deep-fat fryer or chip pan to 185°C.
- Deep fry 10-12 minutes until golden brown. Remove from fat, season and place on a baking tray in a hot oven while you cook fish. This keeps them crispy and removes the need for cooking a second time.

Fish:
- Dripping or oil, for frying
- Plain flour - 400g
- Baking powder - 3 tbs
- Salt - ½ tsp
- Beer - 550ml ice cold
- White fish - 4 pieces

- Heat the fat in a deep-fat fryer or chip pan to 185°C.
- Mix together the flour, baking powder and salt, then quickly whisk in the beer to make a thick paste.
- Dip a piece of fish into the batter, then carefully lower it into the hot fat, and shake the frying basket to prevent the fish sticking to it. Fry one or two pieces at a time: don't overcrowd the fryer.
- Deep fry the fish for about 4-6 minutes, until crisp and golden.
- Lift out of the fat and drain on kitchen paper then serve immediately with the chips.

Stuffed Haddock

Haddock used to be more plentiful and much cheaper than it is now. This recipe from Hartlepool is a great way to serve it without deep frying.

- Haddock - 1 medium size and fresh

stuffing:
- Fresh white breadcrumbs - 300ml
- Parsley - 30g chopped fine
- Suet - 30g grated
- Salt - pinch
- White pepper - pinch
- Milk - to bind
- White flour, a spoonful

- Mix the stuffing to a stiff paste and stuff the fish.
- Sew or tie up and place in a greased pan.
- Shake a little flour over the fish, dot with butter.
- Bake 20 minutes in a hot oven.
- Garnish with slices of lemon and sprigs of curly parsley.
- Serve with plain boiled rice or buttered fingerling potatoes.

Grilled Whole Herring with Durham Mustard

Herring fishing and processing was once a huge employer of transient workers all down the east coast of Scotland and England. There are many old photographs of fish-wives of this fairly recent but now lost industry. These days, herring's most familiar form is as the kipper, but here is a recipe for fresh herring that is easy to prepare. It comes from Cullercoats in Northumberland.

- Fresh whole herrings - 4-6 gutted and scaled
- Durham Mustard - 2 tbs (page 152)
- Lemon juice - 1½ tsp
- Vegetable oil - 1 tbs
- Salt - pinch
- Black pepper - a pinch

(continued over page)

- Make 4 or 5 deep diagonal slashes on the side of each fish and spread the mustard into them.
- Season the herrings with salt and pepper and brush with lemon juice and oil.
- Grill at medium to high heat for 6 minutes a side, turning once.
- Serve with crusty brown bread and lashings of butter.

Yorkshire Fish Cakes

Quite different from the ubiquitous breadcrumbed croquette style of fishcake, these are what I grew up with from the local chippy.

- Large potatoes, peeled and sliced evenly
- White fish, sliced in similar size to the potatoes
- Vinegar batter

Batter

- Place 175g of plain flour and 2 tbs salt in a bowl, make a well in the centre and add 125ml water, 150ml malt vinegar and whisk until smooth. Leave to rest.
- Dust the fish pieces lightly with flour and shake off the excess. Sandwich the pieces of fish between two pieces of potato.
- Dip the cakes into flour and shake off the excess, then dip into the batter to cover well.
- Carefully slip fishcakes one at a time into the hot fat—do not overcrowd. After about 5 minutes they will float. Turn them over, cook for another 5 minutes until golden brown.
- Remove with a slotted spoon and drain well on kitchen paper.
- Serve with chips and mushy peas.

Cured Salmon

This is so simple, yet so good. There are only six ingredients: salmon, salt, pepper, sugar, lime zest and fresh dill. You may double the recipe and sandwich the dill between the flesh of two fillets before wrapping. It is much easier to slice when partially frozen.

- Salmon - 450g fillet (do not use steak), pin-boned

- Coarse salt - 2 tbs non-iodized
- Sugar - 2 tbs
- Black pepper - 2 tsp fresh-ground
- Fresh dill - 1 sprig
- Lime zest - 1 tbs

- Place the salmon on a large piece of plastic wrap (three to four times the length of the fillet) skin side down.
- Mix together the salt, sugar, black pepper and lime zest in a bowl, then place the mixture onto the salmon flesh, making sure to cover all of the exposed area.
- Place the dill on top of the fish.
- Wrap the salmon tightly in plastic wrap. Take a second sheet of plastic wrap and wrap again. Place the package on a large plate or in a plastic container.
- Refrigerate for at least two days—longer will give a more intensified flavour.
- Remove from the refrigerator and rinse off the salmon in cold water. Wipe away any residual salt and pepper and the lime zest and dill from the fish then dry with a paper towel.
- The salmon should be sliced paper-thin on the bias, leaving behind the skin.
- Serve on toasted bread, bagels, or Windermere Crackers (page 148) spread with cream cheese, thin-sliced raw red onion, a few capers and a squeeze of lemon.

Pickled Fish and Fruit

I got this first recipe from an ex-patriot from Cumbria. We were eating raw fish in a sushi bar in Vancouver and he said his mother used to make a posh dish she called 'pickled fish.' I have made it many times and this is an adaptation of it. Where her recipe called for 'fresh fruit' I have been more specific and after some experimentation I give you my favourite version. You can use almost any firm-fleshed fish, but it has to be perfectly fresh. The fish is 'cooked' by the action of the acidic lime juice and you cannot substitute bottled lime juice—it has to be fresh squeezed. The mango is my contribution and it is fit for any company, posh or not.

- Salmon fillet - 250g boned and skinned
- Halibut fillet - 250g boned and skinned
- Small fresh shrimp 250g cleaned and peeled
- Fresh limes - juice of 3
- Vegetable oil - 1 tbs
- Salt - 1 tsp
- Large firm tomatoes - 4 peeled, seeded and diced
- Ripe mango - 1 peeled and diced

- Cut the salmon and halibut into strips measuring about 50mm long by 10mm wide and lay in a shallow dish with shrimp.
- Pour the lime juice over the fish and shrimp, turning to coat well in the juice. Cover with plastic wrap and leave for 1 hour.
- Mix all the other ingredients together and set aside.
- After an hour, season the fish and shrimp with salt, add the oil and mix well in, then replace the cover. Leave to marinate in the fridge for 30 minutes more.
- Divide the fruit mixture into 6 small cold bowls, spoon the fish on top and serve.

Halibut Cured in Rhubarb

This pretty dish is the Northern Counties' answer to sushi. If your rhubarb is not particularly red, you may cheat a little and add a tablespoon of the vinegar from a jar of pickled beetroot.

- Halibut - 1 very fresh fillet, boned and skinned
- Red rhubarb - 250g
- Sugar - 1 tsp
- Salt - ¼ tsp

- Whiz rhubarb, sugar and salt in a blender. Pour over fish in glass dish, cover and refrigerate for about three days.
- Slice and serve with cold sliced potatoes and spinach leaves.

Potted Fish and Fish Paste (see page 99)

Northern Counties Fish Pie

The ubiquitous fish pie was a family dinner for Fridays when I was growing up. It's a homely dish, and one of the great comfort foods of years past. Many families made it with a mashed potato topping, but I liked it best with a flaky pastry crust.

- Firm white fish - 1.5kg
- Plain flour - 14g
- Flaky or puff pastry - 200g
- Butter - 2 tbs
- Salt and pepper
- Hot water - 100ml

for the forcemeat:
- Fresh breadcrumbs - 50g
- Butter - 6 tbs
- Chopped parsley - 1 tbs
- Onion - ½ chopped
- Eggs - 2 beaten
- Thyme -1 tsp
- Salt and sugar

- Wash and dry the fish and cut it into pieces.
- Mix the flour with salt, pepper and parsley, and coat the fish in it.
- Place the fish in a pie dish with hot water and dab butter on top.
- To make the forcemeat, mix the breadcrumbs, softened butter, onion and herbs with the eggs and seasoning.
- Cover the fish with a layer of forcemeat.
- Roll out the pastry and cut off a strip. Wet the inside edge of the pie dish and press the strip of pastry around it.
- Brush the strip with water and lay the lid on top, pressing round the edge, and marking it with a fork.
- Cut a hole in the centre of the pie.
- Glaze the lid and bake at 200°C for 35-40 minutes.

Crab and Leek Quiche

Crab and leeks are two regional favourites combined into this creamy quiche (or pie, as we say in these parts).

- Shortcrust pastry - 225g (page 118)
- Crab meat - 175g
- Leeks - 100g white part only, cleaned and chopped
- Butter - 15g
- Fish stock - 300ml
- Lemon juice - ½ tsp
- Salt - pinch
- Cayenne pepper - pinch
- Eggs - 3
- Double cream - 120ml
- Crab meat - 175g

- Pre-heat oven to 190°C.
- Roll out pastry and line a 20cm flan ring.
- Prick the pastry, cover it with greaseproof paper and fill with rice or dried beans and bake blind for 10 minutes.
- Remove the rice and paper and let cool.
- Par-boil leeks in salted water until soft (about 10 minutes).
- Drain and place in a frying pan.
- Add the butter and stir over a high heat for 2 minutes.
- Beat together the eggs and cream in a bowl.
- Bring the fish stock to the boil and reduce to about 25ml.
- Add the lemon juice, salt and cayenne pepper, then add to egg and cream mixture.
- Line the pastry case with the leeks and spread crab meat over the top. Pour over the eggs and cream mixture and bake in the oven for 20 minutes. Serve this either hot or cold.

Seafood Sausage—(see page 102)

BEEF

History of Shorthorn Cattle

The Northern Counties has had cattle for at least two thousand years, as there is evidence that the short-horned ox was found in Britain at the time of the Roman invasion. Later, the Saxons and Danes introduced cattle from northern Europe. By the late 16th century, superior short-horned cattle flourished. An ancient herd of wild cattle survives at Chillingham, in Northumberland. Reduced to twelve animals in 1947, there is now a second herd in Scotland.

Early breeders of Shorthorn, or Teeswater, cattle developed larger animals, with wide backs and deep, wide forequarters. They were excellent milkers and readily laid on fat when fed well. The Colling brothers, Charles and Robert, are often credited with founding the Shorthorn breed and developing the first systematic breeding program. Charles Colling lived at Ketton Farm, Brafferton, about four miles northeast of Darlington, in County Durham. Robert Colling lived at Barmpton, a mile farther south. About 1783 the Colling brothers met with Richard Bakewell, the visionary livestock breeder, and incorporated some of his breeding methods. In 1796 they successfully bred the fabled 'Durham Ox.' This enormous beast was exhibited all over the country and reached a weight of 3,400 pounds. Nearly all shorthorns in Canada, the United States and Great Britain today trace to their ancestry back to the Colling brothers' herds.

Much beef today is imported from overseas, but for those who want the best, it's still possible to find home-grown cuts from the plains of the east coast where Northumberland, Durham and North Riding farmers follow the same high standards of husbandry as their forebears of the past two thousand years.

Sirloin Steak with Durham Mustard—Serves 4

Beef and mustard are a traditional pair. Durham Mustard gives a superb flavour. If you can't make it, use a good whole grain mustard.

- Durham Mustard - 50g (page 152)
- Plain flour - 40g
- Sirloin steaks - 4 x 175g
- Fresh parsley - 2 tbs, chopped
- Fresh thyme - 2 tbs, chopped

- Mix together the mustard and flour, then spread on each steak.
- Line a grill pan with foil, sprinkle with herbs and put the steaks on top. Turning steaks every 2 minutes, grill for 5-15 minutes depending on how well done you like your steak.
- Serve immediately with baked, mashed or fried potatoes.

Pot Roasted Beef

The slow cooker is ideal for making this dish.

- Topside or silverside of beef - 1.25 - 1.5 kg
- Vegetable oil - 4 tbs
- Butter - 25g
- Onions - 2 large quartered
- Carrots - 2 large cut into 1cm slices
- Bunch of herbs - 1
- Black peppercorns - 4
- Salt - ½ tsp
- Red wine - 150ml mixed with 450ml water
- Cornflour - 2 tsp

- Heat the oil and butter in a flameproof casserole dish, add the beef and turn it slowly until browned all over.
- Reduce the heat and pack the vegetables all round the beef. Add the bunch of herbs, peppercorns and salt. Pour in the wine and water.
- Closely cover the casserole with foil and then add its lid and cook at 150°C for 3 hours, until the beef is tender and cooked through.
- Transfer the beef to a heated serving dish. Discard the bunch of herbs. Lift out the vegetables with a slotted spoon and place around the beef. Keep hot while making the sauce.
- Bring the cooking liquid in the casserole dish to the boil. Mix the cornflour with a little water to make a smooth paste, and pour into the boiling gravy in the casserole dish, stirring constantly. Pour the sauce over the beef and vegetables and serve.

Veal with Mustard

Also known as veal collops—a collop is a thick slice of any boneless red meat cut across the grain and beaten flat.

- Veal collops - 2 at 125g each, pounded 5mm thick
- Flour for dredging the veal
- Butter - 4 tbs

(continued over page)

- Shallots - 1 tbs minced
- Dry white wine - 135ml
- Durham Mustard - 2 tbs (page 152)
- Fresh basil - small bunch chopped
- Unsalted butter - 2 tbs cold cut into bits.

- Season the veal with salt and pepper and dredge it in the flour, shaking off the excess.
- In a frying pan, heat the butter over moderately high heat until it is hot but not smoking, and fry the veal for 2 minutes on each side, or until it is cooked through, then transfer it to a plate.
- In the fat remaining in the frying pan cook the shallots until they are softened, add the wine and deglaze the frying pan, scraping up the brown bits.
- Boil the liquid until it is reduced by half then stir in the mustard, the basil, and salt and pepper to taste.
- Remove the pan from the heat and add the cold butter, a little at a time, whisking until the butter is incorporated. Serve the veal with the sauce.

Roast Liver

Roast liver is an enigma – far better than its ingredients suggest it should be. Excellent with Pan Haggerty (page 28).

- Beef liver - 500g in a single piece
- Bacon slices - 250g
- Onion - 1
- Fresh breadcrumbs - 25g
- Egg - 1 beaten
- Hot water
- Mixed herbs - 1 tbs
- Salt & pepper

- Slit a pocket into the liver lengthwise (almost through to the other side).

- Slice a rasher of bacon into small bits and add to finely diced onion, breadcrumbs, herbs, salt and pepper. Mix to form dressing with a little hot water then stuff the pocket and tie up with string.
- Wrap it around with three or four rashers of bacon and place it on a baking tray.
- Bake in a moderate oven 180°C about 45 minutes or until tender.
- Make brown gravy with the fat in the baking dish, or serve with redcurrant jelly.

Beef Casserole

Casserole if it's company, stew if it's family - posh or homely everyone loves them and here we have a fairly generic recipe that is popular in the Northern Counties. An innovative variation from Middlesbrough, it adds a little dry stout right at the end of cooking.

- Stewing beef - 1kg cubed
- Plain flour - 2 tbs
- Vegetable oil - 2 tbs
- Mushrooms - 125g sliced
- Beef stock - 250ml
- Durham Mustard - 2 tbs (page 152)
- Fresh herbs, tied for easy removal thyme, bay, rosemary, parsley
- Salt and pepper to taste
- Dry stout - 150ml (optional)

Preheat oven to 180°C.
- Toss cubed beef in flour then brown in oil in a frying pan. Place in a casserole dish.
- Fry the mushrooms until lightly cooked and add to casserole with combined meat stock and mustard. Stir. Scrape pan and add to casserole. Add salt and pepper.
- Place tied herbs on top of meat, then cover and cook for two hours, stirring once during cooking. Remove herbs and, if you like, stir in the stout just before serving.
- Serve with boiled potatoes and crusty bread to sop up all that delicious gravy.

Beef Roll

Simply a meat loaf with its old fashioned name. An excellent dish hot or cold and easy to cut into thin slices for sandwiches.

- Minced beef - 750g
- Minced ham - 750g
- Fresh breadcrumbs - 300g
- Salt & pepper - pinch of each
- Worcestershire sauce - 1 tbs
- Tomatoes, tinned - 400g

- Mix first 5 ingredients, form into a roll, place in a large loaf pan and bake at 180°C for 40 minutes.
- When done, pour the tomatoes over and put back in oven for a further 15 minutes.
- Serve with potatoes and green vegetables.

The roll may be water-bathed if preferred. Wrap the roll in plastic kitchen film rolled tight into a large sausage, then wrap again in strong foil. Place the roll in a pan half filled with boiling water, cover with more foil and place in the oven at 175°C for one hour. Remove from the water bath and allow to cool completely in the foil, then unwrap and rewrap in fresh plastic wrap and refrigerate until ready to use.

Witton Park Pie

My mother's recipe. This was so popular with my Scots relatives when they came to visit that they always referred to it as 'Witton Park pie.'

Filling:
- Lean stewing beef - 900g cut into generous chunks
- Plain flour - 2 tbs seasoned to taste with salt and pepper
- Onion - 1 large sliced
- Garlic - 1 clove crushed
- Dry stout - 340ml
- Swede - 225g diced small
- Carrots - 225g sliced

- Vegetable oil - 3 tbs
- Fresh lovage - 1 bunch chopped fine

Pre-heat oven to 170°C
- Lightly coat the meat in seasoned flour.
- Heat oil in a large frying pan, add the meat and brown evenly.
- Remove, drain and place in a casserole.
- Add the onions and garlic to the pan and cook for a few minutes until softened but not brown.
- Remove and transfer to the casserole.
- Add 3-4 tbs of stout to the pan, bring to the boil, stirring to extract all of the pan juices.
- Pour into the casserole, add the remaining vegetables, thyme and stout and mix well.
- Cover and cook in the oven for 1½ to 2 hours.

Dumpling Crust:
- Plain flour - 225g
- Buttermilk - 175ml
- Salt - ½ tsp
- Sugar - ½ tsp
- Baking powder - 1 tsp

- Sieve all the dry ingredients into a bowl, mixing well.
- Mix in the buttermilk until the dough comes together it should be sticky but pliable.
- Turn onto a floured board, knead lightly.
- Shape the dough with your hands to fit the casserole (about 2cm thick).
- Remove the casserole from the oven.
- Place the dumpling crust carefully on top of the stew, making sure that it covers the entire surface.
- Replace the casserole lid, return to the oven, increase heat to 200°C and bake for 30-40 minutes. Remove lid for the last 10 minutes to brown the crust.
- Serve with fingerling potatoes or buttered peas.

Durham Pot Pie

These are really just steak and kidney puddings, but they are placed under a grill to brown and crisp the top before serving. This recipe came from a pub in the market place in Durham City where it was offered for lunch and dinner well into the 1970s.

- Stewing steak - 500g cut into 2cm cubes
- Kidney - 200g cored and sliced
- Seasoned flour - 60g
- Onions - 1 peeled and chopped
- Suet pastry - 250g (page 120)
- Beef stock - 250ml
- Parsley - small bunch chopped fine

- Toss the meat in seasoned flour until lightly coated.
- Layer meat alternately with half the onion and half the parsley in a pudding basin.
- Roll out the pastry to be slightly larger than the top of the basin. Lay the pastry on top of the filling so that a lip comes up the inside edge to the top of the basin.
- Tie a piece of buttered parchment paper over the basin, then crimp a second cover of foil over the top of that.
- Steam for 3½ hours in a large pan with a lid in about 500ml water. Top up as necessary.
- Remove from the pan. You may remove the covers and place under a grill to brown the crust. Eat straight out of the basin or serve onto a plate.

Oxtail Brawn (see page 94)

PORK

The modern pig of the Northern Counties is the Yorkshire White, a huge beast often crossed with the Danish Landrace to produce the Large White, the default pig of supermarkets around the world. Modern pigs are bred to be leaner than their ancestors, although the latest science tells us that fat is essential for health, but advertisers say lean is best. Certainly, my experience with cooking pork and making charcuterie says the old breeds are the best. Of our local breeds, the Small Yorkshire, the Bilsdale Blue, and the Cleveland pig are all extinct, and the last Cumberland pig died in 1960 making it impossible to make a truly authentic Cumberland sausage.

Alnwick Stew

A Northumberland dish made from chopped bacon forehock layered with onions and potatoes. Posh Panakelty!

- Onions - 3, chopped
- Bacon, forehock or end collar - 900g cubed about 3-5cm
- Potatoes - 450-675g peeled and sliced
- English mustard powder - to taste
- Black pepper - to taste
- Bay leaf - 1
- Fresh parsley - chopped, for garnish

- Place a layer of onions in the base of a large, heavy-bottomed saucepan, add a layer of bacon and then a layer of sliced potatoes, seasoning each layer with a little mustard and pepper. Continue layering and and finish with a layer of potatoes.
- Place a bay leaf on top and pour in sufficient cold water to come just below the top layer of potatoes.
- Cover with a lid, bring to the boil, then simmer very gently for 1-1½ hours.

Serve the stew garnished with chopped parsley and accompanied by boiled carrots.

Gissies—Serves 4

I can only think these are called Gissies because they're made of pork—the north country name for pigs.

- Pork steaks - 4
- Butter - 115g
- White breadcrumbs - 100g
- Sausage meat - 115g
- Fresh sage - 1 tbs
- Dry cider or white wine - 240ml
- Salt & pepper

- Beat the pork steaks until paper-thin.
- Mix breadcrumbs, sausage meat and sage. Spread this mixture over each pork steak, roll up and secure with a toothpick.
- Put Gissies in a greased shallow dish and add the wine or cider.
- Bake in a moderate oven, 180°C for about 45 minutes.

Serve with glazed carrots and mashed potato.

Bacon Chops in Gooseberry Sauce—Serves 4

Gooseberries are a perfect match for pork.

- Soft brown sugar - 1 tbs
- Durham Mustard - 1 tbs (page 152)
- Bacon chops - 4 weighing about 175g each
- Butter - 15g
- Onion - 1 large, chopped
- Chicken stock - 150ml
- Gooseberries - 110g topped and tailed

- Mix together the brown sugar and Durham Mustard and rub into both sides of the chops.
- Melt the butter in a large frying pan. Cook the onion for 2 minutes, then add the bacon chops, half the stock and the gooseberries. Simmer gently for 15 minutes.
- Remove the chops. Blend the onions and gooseberries until smooth.
- Return the chops, gooseberries and onions to the pan with the remaining stock. Simmer gently for 10 minutes, until the chops are tender and cooked through.

Serve with sliced green beans or Cumbrian cabbage (page 29).

Bacon Cuddies

Similar to Devils on Horseback (kidneys wrapped in bacon and grilled) and Angels on Horseback (scallops wrapped in bacon and grilled), these bacon-wrapped sausages disappear quickly at festive gatherings. There's an equine connection in the name too … cuddy was the name given to the small ponies that worked alongside coal miners.

- Fresh breadcrumbs - 50g
- Onion - 1 minced
- Egg - 1 lightly beaten
- Fresh sage - 1 tbs finely shredded
- Sausage meat - 500g
- Smoky bacon - 12 rashers, no rind

- Make a stuffing of breadcrumbs, minced onion, egg, and sage.
- Beat the bacon slices and roll with a rolling pin until they are doubled in size.
- Divide sausage meat into 12 pieces and form each piece into a cup shape with the fingers.
- Insert a good spoonful of stuffing and massage the meat up until it closes over the top and smooth over the join.
- Wrap one of the extended rashers of bacon rashers around each sausage meat ball several times so that it is completely covered.
- Place rasher-end down on a baking tray.
- Bake in a medium oven for 1 hour.

Pickled Pork

Pickled pork is another name for an unsmoked bacon joint. Once a popular dish in the Northern Counties, traditionally served with pease pudding and mustard.

- Bacon joint, shoulder or hand - 1.5 kg soaked for 4 hours
- Water - 2 litres
- Onions - 4 large chopped
- Carrots - 6 large cut in half lengthwise
- Lovage - 4 tbs chopped
- Small turnips - 4 halved
- Black peppercorns - 6
- Coriander seeds - 1 tbs
- Fresh parsley - 1 sprig
- Fresh thyme - 1 sprig

- Put the pork and water in a large saucepan and bring to the boil.
- Add the remaining ingredients and simmer for about 1½ hours.
- Place the pork and vegetables on a warm serving dish and serve with Pease Pudding (page 39) and Durham Mustard (page 152).

Pork Fillet in Durham Mustard Cream Sauce — Serves 4

A rich dish combining the best of Northern Counties ingredients - pork, mustard and cream.

- Pork fillet or tenderloin - 700g cut in 1.5cm slices
- Butter - 5g
- Vegetable oil - 1 tbs
- Garlic clove - 1 crushed
- Dry white wine - 150ml
- Sour cream - 150ml
- Durham Mustard - 2 tbs (page 152)

- Flatten each piece of pork with a rolling pin or meat mallet.
- Heat the butter and oil in a large frying pan and fry the garlic for 1 minute without browning, then remove and discard.

- Add the meat and brown on all sides.
- Add the wine and stir to incorporate the sediment from the bottom of the pan, then add the sour cream and mustard.
- Stir the meat with the sauce and cook for 2-3 minutes and serve.
- Serve with Butter Barley (page 38).

Gateshead Floddies

Served with sausages and eggs for breakfast, floddies are traditional to Tyneside.

- Potatoes - 225g peeled
- Onions, 2 medium, peeled
- Streaky bacon (no rind) - 175g chopped fine
- Self-raising flour - 50g
- Salt and black pepper
- Eggs - 2 beaten
- Bacon fat - 40g

- Grate the potatoes, rinse, drain well and place in a bowl.
- Grate or finely chop the onions and add to the potatoes with the bacon, flour and seasoning. Mix well.
- Stir in the beaten eggs.
- Heat the bacon fat in a large frying pan.
- Drop tablespoons of the mixture carefully into the pan and fry steadily for 5-8 minutes, turning once, until golden brown and cooked through.
- Drain on kitchen paper and keep hot until ready to serve.

Pork and Pear Loaf (see page 93)

Roast Pork Loin—Serves many

Simple, but delicious, this features often at Sunday dinner all over the Northern Counties.

- Loin of pork - 1 (with skin)
- Coriander seeds - 20g crushed

- Coarse salt - 25g
- Fresh-ground black pepper

- Dry the skin, score all over and rub in the herbs and salt.
- Roast 15-20 minutes at 210°-220°C, then 25 minutes per 500g at 160°-170°C.

Serve with roast potatoes, Yorkshire pudding (page 197) and gravy.

Orchard Pork

An Autumnal dish that is so good it can be served any time of year.

- Pork shoulder steaks - 500g cut thin
- Large onion - 1 sliced thin
- Large cooking apple - 1 peeled, cored and sliced thin
- Cider vinegar -125ml
- Salt and pepper

- Melt 1 tbs fat at high heat in a lidded deep frying pan.
- Add the pork a few steaks at a time and brown on both sides. Remove from pan and keep to one side.
- Add the onion and apple slices to the pan, then put the pork back in on top of the slices.
- Add cider, salt and pepper and put the lid on the frypan.
- Cook gently for about an hour. Adjust seasoning to taste. At this point you may wish to add a little cream to the sauce which will have accumulated, and perhaps a tablespoon of Durham Mustard (page 152).

Serve with boiled and buttered new potatoes and Braised Red Cabbage (page 30).

Pork Bites

These little delicacies were originally just the scraps of pork left over after a pig had been killed and butchered at a smallholding or farm. I was told by the Sunderland butcher that the best part to use was 'owt that's fatty,' so I make mine with pork shoulder, which is about 70% lean and 30% fat. These are so good they could be served as posh hors d'oeuvres if you kept quiet regarding their humble beginnings. Bet you can't eat just one …

- Pork shoulder -1kg
- Garlic powder - 2 tbs
- Onion powder - 1½ tbs
- Salt - 1 tsp
- White pepper - ½ tsp
- Plain flour - 100g
- Cornflour - 30g

- Oil for deep frying

- Cut the pork shoulder into bite size pieces.
- Season the pork bites with the garlic powder, onion powder, salt, pepper.
- Place in a plastic bag with the plain flour and cornflour. Toss well to coat each piece.
- Heat a deep fryer to 175°C. If you don't have a deep fryer you can use a large frying pan or deep pot. You will need to cook in batches so they don't stick together.
- Place the coated pork bites into the deep fryer basket, separated from each other to ensure even cooking
- Lower into the fryer cook and cook for 3-4 minutes until the outsides are crisp and just brown.
- Remove and shake the basket, and pour the cooked bites onto a plate with paper towels to soak up any excess oil.
- Serve warm with a squirt of lemon juice.

LAMB

The Herdwick and the Rough Fell are indigenous sheep of the western side of the Pennine Hills, while the Swaledale, Teeswater and Masham breeds are more common on the eastern side. The North Country Mule is a cross breed from a Swaledale mother, and is common throughout the Northern Counties. The Cheviot takes its name from the hills of Northumberland and is the most common breed in that county. I have been delighted to hear its name pronounced 'shev-ee-oh' in Western Canada.

Mutton, the meat of a fully grown sheep, (a lamb is eight months or younger) was once common but is not produced in any quantity any longer. It can still occasionally be bought, especially in the Lake District, where it usually comes from Herdwick sheep. Many of our regional dishes are lamb based.

Slow-roasted Lamb

- Leg of lamb (about 2.3 kg)
- Large onion, large carrot, stalk of celery - 1 of each all roughly chopped
- Sprigs of fresh rosemary - 3 or 4
- Garlic cloves - 2 crushed
- Sea salt - 1 tbs
- Black pepper - 1 tbs freshly ground
- Vegetable oil - 2 tbs

- Pre-heat the oven to 160°C. Put the lamb on top of the scattered chopped vegetables in a roasting tin and rub it all over with the garlic. Pour the oil evenly over the roast and season with salt and pepper.
- Poke a few holes in the lamb and insert sprigs of rosemary.
- Pour in 250ml water, then cover the roasting tin with a tent of tin foil. Roast for about three hours, then remove the tin foil and open roast for 10 minutes.
- Place the roast on a plate and keep warm.
- Mash the vegetables from the roasting pan through a sieve and make gravy from the pan juices.

The lamb should pull apart, or you can simply slice it and serve with gravy, new potatoes and peas.

Hamsterley Lamb Shanks—Serves 4

- Lamb shanks - 4 about 450g each
- Plain flour - for dusting
- Vegetable oil - 1 tbs
- Garlic - 4 cloves, chopped
- Wild mushrooms - 450g
- Red wine - 250ml
- Lamb stock - 500ml
- Fresh rosemary - 1 tbs chopped
- Salt and pepper to taste

- Dredge the lamb shanks in the flour.
- In a large frying pan over high heat, heat the vegetable oil until smoking hot. Add the lamb shanks and brown well, 4-5 minutes per side. Place in a roasting pan.
- Add the garlic and mushrooms to fry pan and fry until the mushrooms are tender, 3-4 minutes.
- Add the wine and cook for another 3-4 minutes, or until the wine has evaporated.
- Add the stock and bring the mixture to a boil over high heat. Add the rosemary, salt and pepper to taste, then pour everything over the lamb shanks in the roasting pan.
- Cover the roasting pan with a lid or tin foil and place in preheated oven 200°C. Bake until the lamb is tender, 1 to 1½ hours.

Serve the lamb shanks with the wild mushroom sauce, Butter Barley (page 38) or small roasted potatoes.

North York Moors Lamb and Barley Stew

Lamb grazed on the open expanse of the North York Moors on heather tips and wild herbs is particularly tasty and pearl barley is the natural ingredient to accompany it in stews and casseroles.

- Leg or shoulder of lamb - 1.4 kg, boned, trimmed and cubed
- Plain flour - 2 tbs
- Streaky bacon - 3 rashers, chopped
- Butter - 25g
- Onions - 2 medium, chopped
- Carrots - 2 medium, sliced
- Turnip or swede - 110g, diced
- Celery - 2 sticks, diced
- Pearl barley - 2 tbs
- Fresh herbs such as thyme, rosemary, parsley - 2 tsp, chopped
- Lamb or beef stock - 300ml
- Fresh parsley - chopped for garnish

(continued over page)

- Toss the lamb in the flour.
- Fry the bacon crisp and set aside. Add the butter and lamb to the fry pan and fry until browned all over. Remove lamb and set aside.
- Add the onions, carrots, turnip or swede and celery to the fry pan and fry for 5-10 minutes until they are beginning to brown.
- Place all ingredients into a large casserole, add the pearl barley and herbs and pour in the stock.
- Bring to the boil, then cover and simmer for 2 hours, stirring occasionally to prevent it sticking, until the lamb is tender.

Serve with mashed potato and Cumbrian Cabbage (page 39).

Leg of Lamb Roasted with Raspberry Basting Sauce

The slightly sweet basting sauce complements the flavour of lamb. The recipe comes from the Lake District and mirrors the flavours of Cumberland sauce.

- Leg of lamb - about 3kg
- Salt and freshly ground black pepper to taste
- Garlic clove - 1 crushed
- Dry red wine - 250ml
- Raspberry jam - 100ml seedless
- Orange juice - 100ml

- Pour half the red wine over the lamb. Season the leg with salt, pepper, and garlic, rubbing the spices into the meat. Marinate for at least 2 hours.
- Preheat the oven to 230°C. Make the basting sauce by stirring together the raspberry jam, orange juice, and remaining wine.
- Put the lamb from the marinade into a roasting pan, reserve the marinade.
- Place the roasting pan into the hot oven for 15 minutes to sear the meat. Lower the oven temperature to 175°C, pour the marinade over the lamb, and continue to cook for 1½ hours, or 35 minutes per kilo. After roasting for 20 minutes at 175°C, pour the basting sauce over the lamb and continue to baste every 15-20 minutes. Add extra wine if you run low on basting sauce.

- When the lamb is done, remove to a platter, tent with foil and let sit for 10 minutes before carving.

Serve with the pan juices, roast potatoes and peas.

Old Fashioned Hot Pot

Beef or pork may be substituted for the mutton.

• Neck or loin of mutton - 750g
• Potatoes - 500g
• Large onion - 1
• Stock - 200ml
• Dripping 30g
• Parsley - small handful chopped
• Mixed herbs - pinch
• Salt - to taste
• Pepper - to taste

- Wash, peel and slice potatoes, peel and slice onions.
- Lightly fry potatoes and onions separately.
- Cut the mutton into bite-size pieces and lightly fry in dripping.
- Line a casserole with alternate layers of potatoes, onions and meat, seasoning well and add a pinch of mixed herbs.
- Moisten with stock, cover and cook at 230°C for 1½ hours.
- Remove any fat before serving and sprinkle with chopped parsley.
- Mushrooms or peas may be added 10 minutes before serving.

Northern Counties Roast Lamb

- Leg of lamb - 3 kg
- Salt and pepper - to taste
- Red potatoes - 12 quartered
- Mixed dried herbs - 1 tbs
- Rosemary sprigs - 6
- Vegetable oil - 2 tbs
- Coarse salt - 1 tbs
- Orange marmalade - 100ml
- Mustard seeds - 1 tbs
- Dried thyme - 2 tsp

- Toss the potatoes with oil, salt and dried herbs, place in the roasting pan then put a rack in the pan and place lamb leg on it.
- Season lamb with salt and pepper to taste.
- Roast at 165°C for 35 minutes per kilo.
- Combine orange marmalade, mustard seeds and thyme. Halfway through roasting, baste lamb with marmalade mixture.
- Roast to desired degree of doneness. When lamb is done, open the oven and let it stand for 15 minutes before slicing.

Serve with the roasted potatoes.

Herbed Rack of Lamb—Serves 4

- Racks of lamb - 2 trimmed of fat
- Durham Mustard - 2 tbs (page 152)
- Yorkshire Relish - 2 tbs (page 164)
- Garlic - 2 large cloves, crushed
- Dried rosemary - 1 tsp
- Ground ginger - ½ tsp
- Dried thyme - 1 tsp
- Ground marjoram - 1 tsp
- Freshly ground black pepper to taste
- Vegetable oil - 2 tbs

- Whisk together the Durham Mustard, Yorkshire Relish, garlic, herbs, spices, and oil.
- Paint the marinade generously over the lamb, place in a roasting pan and let marinate at room temperature for 1 hour.
- Roast the lamb in a preheated 200°C oven for 25 minutes for medium-rare. Remove to a platter, carve the rack and present.

Serve with new potatoes and Spring greens.

Shepherd's Pie

There must be a million recipes for shepherd's pie. Some say it should be made with lamb, some say beef ... some say use raw meat, some cooked. Some say it should have a topping of cheese, some say that makes it a cottage pie. Here is mine, I think it's the best in the world.

- Cold, finely-diced, slow-braised mutton - 450g
Gravy:
- Plain flour - 25g
- Butter - 25g
- Lamb or beef stock, about 250ml
- Cream - 125ml
- Hot, smooth-mashed potatoes - 700g

- Place the diced lamb in an ovenproof pie dish.
- Melt the butter in a pan, add the flour and mix together. Stir for several minutes until it begins to turn brown, then add stock while stirring to make a smooth gravy. Add cream and bring to the boil.
- Pour the gravy over the lamb, smooth the mash over the top and place in the oven for 10 minutes to brown. If you don't care whether it's brown or not, you can just microwave a few minutes.

Sweet Mutton Pies (see page 104)

Lap of Lamb

A recipe from the wonderful Brydon family of Hebburn on Tyne. With special thanks to Stephen, who tested my creations without complaint for years and years, and whose educated palate and diplomatic honesty are much appreciated.

- Lamb breast - 1, about 1kg skinned and boned
- Salt - 1 tsp
- Black pepper - 1 tsp
- Fresh rosemary - 2 tbs chopped fine
- Onion - 1 large peeled and quartered
- Carrot - 4 split in half
- Vegetable oil - 1 tbs
- Stock or dry cider - 250ml

- Season the inside of the breast generously with salt and pepper. Sprinkle over the rosemary and roll up tight. Tie with string.
- Oil the outside of the roll and place the lamb onto a bed of onions and carrots in a shallow roasting pan.
- Add the stock or cider, cover the pan with foil and cook in a 135°C oven for 2 hours.
- Remove the foil and cook for a further 30 minutes until meat is very tender.
- Make a thin gravy from the remaining stock and juices. Serve with minted new potatoes and peas.

POULTRY

There was a time when chicken wasn't the inexpensive and ubiquitous poultry on the table every Sunday. In times past, only farmers and those who kept hens on allotments and smallholdings got to have chicken with anything like regularity. That changed with modern farming methods and nowadays the other forms of poultry are the more rare and often only available in restaurants during the shooting season. But you can make them all at home!

Durham Chicken — 4 servings

- Chicken breast halves - 4 boneless, skinless
- Durham Mustard - 4 tbs (page 152)
- Orange juice - 3 tbs
- Salt - ½ tsp
- Honey - 3 tbs
- Black pepper - ¼ tsp
- Vegetable oil - 1 tbs oil
- Fresh spinach - two good handfuls, rinsed and well-drained

- Mix mustard, orange juice, and honey in small bowl, set aside.
- Season the chicken with salt and pepper and cook 10-12 minutes in a large frying pan.
- Remove chicken when cooked through and lightly browned.
- Add spinach and cook until slightly wilted. Place onto plate and top with chicken breasts—keep them warm.
- Pour the honey mixture into the frying pan and heat through, stirring constantly. Pour over the chicken and spinach and serve immediately.

Chicken in Brown Ale — Serves 4

Don't worry too much about the large amount of garlic—when boiled or baked, it loses its bite and becomes mild and sweet. Serve with pan-fried potatoes flavoured with onions and herbs. Newcastle Brown Ale is the beer of choice, but any brown ale will do.

- Chicken breasts - 4 skin on
- Brown ale - 250ml
- Mushrooms - 100g quartered
- Swiss cheese - 100g shredded
- Garlic - 1 head peeled and left whole

- Wash and pat dry the chicken and season with salt and pepper.

- Place in a grill pan and brown under the grill for about 5 minutes per side, or until well browned. Set aside and keep warm.
- While the chicken is grilling, boil the head of garlic in water for about 20 minutes. Drain, cool and peel the individual cloves, then scatter them around the chicken, add the wine and mushrooms to the pan, and bake in a 200°C oven for 10 minutes.
- Sprinkle the shredded cheese on top of the chicken, lower heat to 190°C, and bake for another 10-15 minutes or until done.

Lindisfarne Chicken — Serves 4

"The Holy Island of Lindisfarne is well known for mead. In the medieval days when the monks inhabited the island, it was thought that if the soul was in God's keeping, the body must be fortified with this elixir of herbs and honey, the wine bequeathed to posterity as Lindisfarne Mead. The monks have long vanished, but their spirit lingers in this aphrodisiac whose exact recipe remains a secret of the family still producing it. The word 'honeymoon' is derived from the ancient Norse custom of having newly-weds drink mead for a whole moon in order to increase their fertility and therefore chances of a happy and fulfilled marriage."

- Chicken pieces - 4
- Vegetable oil - 2 tbs
- Butter - 1 tbs
- Onion - 1 small, chopped
- Mushrooms - 110g sliced
- Fresh parsley - 2 tbs chopped fine
- Lemon juice - 1 tsp
- Lindisfarne mead - 150ml
- Salt and black pepper - to taste

- Preheat the oven to 190°C.
- In a frying pan, brown the chicken pieces in the oil and butter. Place into a casserole dish.
- Add the chopped onion to the oil and butter in the pan and fry for 2-3 minutes. Add the mushrooms, parsley, lemon juice, mead and seasonings.

- Stir well and cook for a further 3 minutes before pouring the sauce over the chicken pieces.
- Cover and cook in the oven for about 1 hour.

Pickaree

A great recipe for newly gathered wild mushrooms from the woods of the Northern Counties. I first made his one-pot dish using chanterelles picked from a sworn-to-secret spot in County Durham, but you can use any earthy mushroom available from the grocery in the Autumn. The name comes from mushroom 'picker.' You may also make this with pearl barley instead of rice.

- Chicken thighs - 8
- Vegetable oil - 1 tbs
- Raw rice - 185g
- Chicken stock - 1 litre
- Carrot - 1 diced
- Celery - 1 stalk, diced
- Onion - 1 diced
- Tomatoes - 4 small diced
- Wild mushrooms - 250g sliced

- In a large saucepan, fry the onions, carrots and celery in the oil until cooked. Remove from the pan and set aside.
- Add the chicken thighs to the pan skin side down and cook until skin is brown and crisp.
- Return the vegetables and add the tomatoes and raw rice, then add the chicken stock and bring to a boil.
- Reduce heat, cover with lid and cook on low heat for 30 minutes.

Glossy Duck with Pop-Ally Onions and Pear Hash

- Duck breasts - 4 skin on
- Vegetable oil - 2 tbs
- Ripe pears - 2 cored, cut into 1cm cubes
- Pearl onions - about 20, blanched and peeled
- Potatoes - 4 peeled, boiled until just tender, cut into chunks

- Fresh sage - 2tbs chopped
- Chicken broth - 150ml
- Fig balsamic vinegar - 100ml

- Score duck skin in grid pattern and season generously with salt and pepper.
- Heat oil in large frying pan over medium-high heat. Add the duck and cook about 6 minutes per side for medium. Transfer to cutting board. Cover with foil.
- Discard all but 2 tbs fat from frying pan. Heat fat over high heat then add the pears, onions, and potatoes. Fry until beginning to brown, about 5 minutes.
- Stir in sage; season with salt and pepper. Transfer hash to bowl and cover to keep warm.
- Reheat the frying pan over high heat and add the broth and vinegar. Bring to the boil, scraping up all the browned bits. Reduce to glaze, then season with salt and pepper.
- Divide hash among plates. Cut duck into 15cm-thick slices; fan over hash. Drizzle glaze over and serve.

Derwentwater Duck with Cumberland Sauce — Serves 4

Game flourishes on the moors and lakes of the North and the wild duck of Derwentwater are especially valued for their tenderness and flavour. You can, of course, use any other duck for this recipe. The rich flavour is complemented by the sweet sharp flavour of Cumberland Sauce.

- Duck portions - 4
- Orange - 1 large, zest and juice
- Lemon - 1 zest and juice
- Redcurrant jelly - 4 tbs
- Cornflour - 2 tsp
- Port - 4 tbs
- Brandy - 2 tbs
- Watercress and orange slices to garnish

- Prick the duck portions all over with a sharp skewer or fork. Place on a wire rack over a roasting tin. Roast in pre-heated 190°C

oven for 45-60 minutes until skin is crisp and the juices run clear when the thickest part of the duckling is pricked with a skewer.
- Put the orange and lemon juices in a small saucepan, add the zests, cover and simmer gently for 5 minutes.
- Add the redcurrant jelly and let it melt slowly over a gentle heat. Mix the cornflour with the port, then stir into the sauce and bring to the boil, stirring until the sauce thickens.
- When the duckling portions are cooked put them on a warmed serving dish and keep hot while the sauce is finished. Pour off the fat from the tin, leaving the juices behind, then add the brandy and stir over a gentle heat to stir in the sediment from the bottom of the tin.
- Add the sauce and stir well. Serve with the duckling. Garnish with sprigs of watercress and orange slices.

Roast Duck with Stuffing

- Ducks - 2 dressed
- Lemon juice - 2 tbs
- Celery - 2 stalks chopped
- Onion - 1 diced
- Dry breadcrumbs - 230g
- Butter - 170g
- Salt - 1½ tsp
- Black pepper - 1¼ tsp
- Chicken stock - 250ml
- Thyme - ½ tsp

- Make the stuffing by cooking the celery and onion in a frying pan with butter until onion becomes limp, then combine the bread crumbs, ½ tsp salt, ¼ tsp pepper, thyme and enough stock to obtain the consistency you like best.
- Rub ducks inside and out with the remaining butter, salt, pepper and lemon juice then stuff the ducks and wrap them in foil.
- Place the ducks in a 165°C oven and bake for 1½ hours, then remove the foil and baste them with margarine. Bake uncovered another ½ hour, or until the ducks become golden brown.

Michaelmas Goose with Apples and Prunes

'Green' geese, which had fed on pasture, made a traditional feast for Michaelmas in late September, and were less fatty than Christmas geese. In Ireland and northern England, it was thought that if you ate goose at Michaelmas you would have good luck for the rest of the year. The roast bird was always accompanied by apples, as windfalls were plentiful.

- Oven-ready goose with giblets - about 4-5 kg
- Butter - 15g
- Onion - 1 large, chopped
- Prunes - 450g soaked
- Port - 4 tbs
- Fresh sage - 1 tbs chopped
- Fresh breadcrumbs - 100g
- Apples - 6 cored and cut into 8 wedges
- Dry white wine - 300ml

- Prick the goose all over with a sharp skewer or fork. Remove the inside fat and reserve.

Stuffing:
- Melt butter in a large frying pan, onion and cook 5-6 minutes, until soft. Chop the goose liver and giblets fine, then add to the onion and cook gently for 2-3 minutes.
- Chop half the prunes roughly and stir into the onion with the port. Cover and simmer gently for 5 minutes. Add the sage and breadcrumbs and mix thoroughly.
- Spoon the stuffing into the neck end of the goose, then truss.
- Put the bird on a wire rack in a roasting tin. Cover the breast with the reserved fat then with foil. Roast at 200°C for 30 minutes per kilo plus 15 minutes, basting frequently.
- 30 minutes before the end of cooking time, drain off fat and discard. Add apples to roasting tin with the remaining prunes. Add the wine. Place the bird on top, standing on the roasting rack. Remove the foil and fat and cook, uncovered, for the last 30 minutes. Serve with boiled potatoes and Braised Red Cabbage (page 30).

Pigeon Casserole — Serves 4

- Pigeons - 4 split down back
- Salt and flour
- Margarine - 2 tbs
- Mushrooms - 200g
- Dried parsley - 2 tsp
- Dry white wine - 150ml

- Salt and dust pigeons with flour. Fry in margarine until brown. Place in a casserole and pour pan drippings over the birds.
- Add mushrooms and parsley. Pour enough wine in casserole to half cover birds. Cover casserole and bake at 180°C for one hour.

Baked Quail — Serves 4

- Quail - 4 cut in pieces
- Carrots - 4 cut in small chunks
- Celery - 4 stalks cut in small chunks
- Onion - 1, sliced
- Vegetable oil - 5 tbs
- Plain flour - 3 tbs
- Salt and pepper
- Bay Leaf - 1
- Rosemary - ½ tsp
- Chicken bouillon cube - 1
- Apple juice - 250ml

- Heat oil in a frying pan and brown quail.
- Place quail in casserole dish and top with onion slices, carrots and celery. Add all remaining ingredients to frying pan, bring to boil and simmer 15 minutes.
- Pour over quail and bake in 165°C oven for one hour.

Raby Pheasant — Serves 2

The estate of Lord Barnard provided this recipe, but you'll have to buy your pheasant elsewhere.

- Large oven-ready pheasant - 1
- Butter - 4 tbs
- Salt and black pepper
- Dessert apples - 2 large, peeled, cored and sliced
- Heavy cream - 250ml
- Calvados - 80ml

Preheat oven to 180°C.
- Melt half the butter in a large frying pan. Add the pheasant, season with salt and pepper, and brown it all over. Set aside.
- Melt the remaining butter in the frying pan. Add the apple slices and cook them until golden brown.
- Put a layer of apple slices in a casserole dish big enough to hold the pheasant. Place the bird, breast down, on top of the apple slices, and pack it around with the rest of the apple. Pour in one-third of the cream.
- Cook covered for an hour, turning the bird over after 30 minutes.
- Remove the casserole from the oven and increase the heat to 230°C. Pour the remaining cream and the Calvados over the pheasant. Adjust the seasoning, cover the casserole and return it to the oven for 5 minutes. Serve from the casserole.

Pheasant Pie (see page 109)

Grilled Grouse—Serves 2

This recipe works for partridges too. Use 4 partridges

- Dressed grouse - 2
- Streaky bacon - 4 rashers
- Vegetable oil 2 tbs
- Salt - ½ tsp
- Black pepper - ⅛ tsp
- Paprika - ⅛ tsp

- Split the grouse down the back and press them out flat, then rub them on both sides with oil, salt, pepper and paprika.
- Place the grouse breast-side down in a large grill pan, and put under a preheated grill and let them cook for 15 minutes.
- Take the rack out and turn each grouse breast-side up and drape each one with a bacon strip, then continue to grill until bacon become well done.

RED GROUSE.—*Lagopus Scoticus*

SAUSAGE AND POTTED MEAT

Basic Sausage Making

If you intend to make lots of sausage, you really should get specialized equipment. You can get it online these days without problem. But if you only make sausage now and again, just use what is probably already in your kitchen.

If you don't own a mincer/grinder you will have to buy meat already minced from the butcher. A good old-fashioned butcher will mince meat fine or coarse to your specifications. Or you could just mince with a sharp knife.

Unless you cook your sausages without the skins, you'll need to buy casings. There are natural and artificial casings, also available through your butcher. Stuffing is way easier if you have a proper sausage stuffer, but you can use a pastry bag with a large nozzle too. I've even seen a plastic bag with one corner clipped put to service (... you'll need to enlist help though!) Large bowls are handy, too. If possible, everything should be chilled, so you'll need a fridge.

Finally, you need to be able to measure temperature and weight and volume.

Keep in mind that sausage making requires an extra level of cleanliness so be meticulous in sterilizing all your equipment. Fresh sausage links need to be refrigerated at least 24 hours to allow flavours to blend. Fresh sausage should be eaten within a few days of making, but you can freeze them at -18ºC for up to two months.

My research indicates that almost all sausage in the Northern Counties is the fresh kind, but I have found at least two types that are more like the continental style. One is dry sausage (page 96), which - as the name indicates - needs to be dried, and the other is Newbiggin Farm Sausage (page 87), which for authenticity needs to be smoked.

Cumberland Sausage

A regional speciality, a National treasure.

- Pork shoulder - 450g diced
- Pork belly (rindless) - 450g diced
- White breadcrumbs - 50g
- Salt - 2 tsp
- Black pepper - 1 tsp
- Nutmeg - pinch
- Mace - generous pinch
- Dried marjoram - pinch
- Dried sage - pinch
- Cayenne pepper - generous pinch
- Sausage casing

- Chill the meat before use then mince using a coarse disk (you are looking for something the consistency of beef mince). Add in the breadcrumbs and the seasonings and mix until sticky.
- Fry a little to check the seasoning and adjust if necessary.
- Fill sausage casing—true Cumberland Sausage is made in one long coil. Refrigerate the sausage overnight to let the flavours develop, then cook. This sausage is best baked in the oven in a pan just big enough to hold it. It will try to uncoil as it bakes, so you might want to push a skewer through it first.
- Pre-heat the oven to 180°C and bake for about 35 minutes, basting frequently. Tradition is to serve with red cabbage, mashed potatoes and gravy.

Yorkshire Sausage

This is a relatively new sausage, Yorkshire's answer to the Cumberland and Lincolnshire Sausage. In a county-wide street sampling, over 3,500 people chose this as the the official Yorkshire Sausage.

- Pork shoulder - 3kg
- Pork belly - 1kg
- Pinhead rusk or dried breadcrumbs - 625g
- Salt - 65g
- White pepper - 15g
- Nutmeg - 10g
- Mace - 10g
- Ground coriander - 10g
- Dried parsley - 10g

- Mince the pork through a 5mm mincer plate.
- Add the seasonings and bread/ rusk.
- Add about 500ml water to rehydrate the bread or rusk.
- Mince for a second time.
- Fill into natural casings.

Newbiggin Farm Sausage

These are from County Durham and were traditionally smoked, usually for a half a day up the chimney high above a hardwood fire. This version makes things simpler by using liquid smoke.

- Pork shoulder - 1kg minced
- Beef - 500g minced
- Coarse salt - 45g
- White pepper - 30g
- Dried marjoram - 20g
- Garlic paste - 20g
- Ground coriander - 10g
- Sugar - 10g
- Milk powder - 45g
- Mustard powder - 10g

(continued over page)

- Cold water - 250ml
- Liquid smoke - 1 tbs

- Mix all the ingredients and refrigerate overnight.
- Fill into sausage casings. Cook at 200°C in the oven for 1 hour. At this stage they are ready to eat or you can cool them and gently fry them later. They are great included in a casserole or with Cumbrian Cabbage (page 29).

Bassenthwaite Bangers—makes about 12 links

These are skinless so I'm not convinced they can be true bangers. The recipe came from the village of the same name in Allerdale, Cumbria.

- Pork shoulder - 1kg minced
- Bacon - 250g chopped fine
- Salt - 15g salt
- Paprika - 10g
- White pepper - 3g
- Ground allspice - 2g
- Ground cloves - 2g
- Dried thyme - 2g
- Garlic powder - 2g
- Dry bread crumbs - 60g
- Water - 25ml
- Malt vinegar - 25ml

- Combine spices and bread crumbs.
- Blend in spice mixture, water and vinegar with pork and bacon.
- To shape, squeeze through 2cm hole in pastry bag making links 8cm long.
- Fry about 7 min, turning frequently, or grill about 5 minutes on each side.

Lamb and Leek Sausage

We have to have a lamb sausage or two! The first one has a delicious hint of citrus. The recipe comes from a Farmer's Weekly magazine of the 1950s and was sent in by 'Mrs. Armstrong of Barnard Castle,' so Teesdale gets the accolades for this one. It was a bare-bones recipe (no pun intended) with only the ingredients and an instruction to mix and stuff into skins. I made slight changes to the original by adding pork back fat to reach a 30% fat content. Mrs Armstrong used dry elderberry wine, but you can substitute any dry red.

- Minced lamb - 700g
- Minced pork shoulder - 200g
- Pork back fat - 300g cubed small
- Coarse salt - 30g
- Sugar - 25g
- Leeks - 4 chopped, washed and slowly fried until soft.
- Minced fresh garlic - 2 tbs
- Ground coriander - 1 tbs
- Black pepper - 1 tbs
- Parsley - 1 handful chopped
- Dried thyme - 2 tsp
- Orange zest - grated zest of 3
- Dry red wine - 125ml
- Sausage casings

- Cook the leeks until soft, then cool until cold.
- Mix everything together well and put in the fridge overnight.
- Stuff the casings and twist into links.

These are excellent barbecue sausages, but they grill or fry well too.

Lamb and Rosemary Sausage

This recipe can be made dual-flavour, you can use all mint or all rosemary, or mix both as you like.

- Lamb shoulder - 1kg minced
- Pork back fat - 250g minced
- Rosemary and/or mint leaves - 1 tbs chopped very fine
- Coarse salt - 1½ tsp
- Garlic - 3 cloves chopped fine
- Black pepper - 1 tsp
- Chilled red wine - 125ml   *(continued over page)*

- Mix the ingredients well and stuff into casings.
- Allow the sausages to sit overnight in the fridge to develop flavour then gently fry, grill or barbecue.

FOUR TERRINES

Terrine is just a posh word for meatloaf—usually served cold and accompanied by thin slices of crusty bread or crackers and an assortment of pickles. These recipes from farmhouses around the Northern Counties were popular ways to use up small amounts of meat that otherwise would go into sausages as they make an inexpensive but impressive dish for company. They were often made with a mixture of spices similar to Sunderland spice, but you may substitute any combination you prefer. Bacon is always rindless.

Windermere Terrine

- Streaky bacon - 10 rashers whole
- Streaky bacon - 2 rashers diced
- Spinach - 1 bunch, stalks removed and washed
- Shoulder pork - 500g minced coarse
- Chicken thighs - 350g skinned, boned cut into small cubes
- Fresh sage leaves - 6
- Flat-leaf parsley - 4 tbs
- Fresh thyme leaves - 1 tbs
- Allspice - ½ tsp
- Brandy - 50ml
- Egg - 1 lightly beaten

Preheat oven to 160°C.

- Lay bacon rashers across a 25cm x 7cm x 7cm deep terrine dish or loaf pan, overlapping them slightly and allowing the bacon ends to hang over the edge.

- Pour boiling water over spinach in a bowl and let stand for 1 minute. Drain and rinse in cold water. Squeeze water from spinach then chop fine and return to bowl.
- Add pork, chicken and diced bacon to spinach. Chop fine the sage, parsley and thyme. Add to spinach mixture with allspice, brandy, egg, a teaspoon of salt and freshly ground black pepper. Mix until well combined.
- Press mixture into the bacon-lined terrine dish and fold the overhanging bacon over the top. Cover with a lid or foil. Place into a roasting pan. Pour hot water into roasting pan until water comes half way up the sides of terrine dish.
- Bake for 1 hour. Reduce heat to 140°C and bake for a further 20 minutes or until terrine is cooked through.
- Remove the terrine from the water bath and cool completely at room temperature. Cut a piece of stiff cardboard the same size as the terrine and wrap it in foil, then place it with a heavy jar or something similar on top of the terrine to press it down firmly in the refrigerator overnight.

Morpeth Terrine

Berwick-upon-Tweed
Newcastle-upon-Tyne
Alnwick for white bread
Morpeth for swine.

- Shoulder pork - 600g coarse-minced
- Chicken livers - 250g coarse-chopped
- Butter - 2 tbs
- Small onion - 1 chopped fine
- Garlic - 3 cloves minced
- Brandy - 50ml
- Dry breadcrumbs - 135 g
- Fresh parsley - 1 tbs chopped
- Fresh thyme leaves - 1½ tsp
- Fresh chives - 1½ tsp snipped fine
- Black pepper - ½ tsp   *(continued over page)*

- Salt - 2 tsp
- Sunderland spice - 1 tsp (page 164)
- Eggs - 3
- Streaky bacon - 250g

Preheat the oven to 175°C.

- Melt the butter in a frying pan over medium heat. Add the onions and cook until just soft.
- Add the garlic and cook for an additional minute. Remove from the heat and add the brandy.
- Combine the meats in a large mixing bowl with the onion mixture and remaining ingredients except bacon. Mix thoroughly.
- Using the back of a knife, carefully stretch the bacon to about twice its length and line a terrine or loaf pan with the strips. Allow the ends of the bacon to drape over the sides of the pan.
- Press the meat mixture firmly into the terrine or loaf pan.
- Fold the overhanging bacon strips over the top and sides of the mixture.
- Cover the top with a piece of parchment paper, then with foil.
- Put the terrine in a roasting or baking pan and pour enough boiling water in the pan to come about halfway up the sides of the terrine. Place in the oven and cook for 1 to 2 hours.
- Remove the terrine from the water bath and cool completely at room temperature. Cut a piece of stiff cardboard the same size as the terrine and wrap it in foil, then place it with a heavy jar or something similar on top of the terrine to press it down firmly in the refrigerator overnight.

Pâté

Beef Terrine

This one is what used to be called 'pressed beef' but it looks so terrine-like I think it qualifies here.

- Whole salt beef brisket - about 2kg
- Black pepper corns - 2 tbs
- Coriander seeds - 2 tbs
- Cloves 1/2 tsp, ground
- Bunch of thyme
- Carrots - 2, peeled and split in half
- Onion - 1, cut in quarters
- Celery - 3 sticks, cut in half
- Garlic - 1 bulb, cut in half

- Place all the ingredients in a large pot, cover with cold water and place on a medium heat and simmer for 3-4 hours until beef is very tender and soft. Check the water often and make sure the level stays just above the beef.
- Remove the beef from the pot (keep the stock to make a great beef broth) and carefully shred it using two forks. Reserve the soft fat from the top of the brisket.
- Season to taste—the beef brisket will already be salty so you may only need pepper. Add the reserved fat and mix well this will help to keep the terrine together. Pack a prepared terrine mould tight with the beef. Cover and place in the fridge overnight.
- When set remove and cut into slices.

Serve with your favourite pickles and crusty bread.

Pork and Pear Loaf

A terrine with a homely name that makes an appearance at tea-tables on special occasions. It should be seen more often as it is easy to make and very tasty.

- Pear - 1 cored and chopped coarsely
- Minced pork - 500g
- Fine dry bread crumbs - 100g
- Milk - 200ml   *(continued over page)*

- Egg - 1
- Celery and onion - 2 tbs each minced
- Garlic - ½ clove minced
- Fresh-ground pepper - ⅛ tsp
- Ground sage - ½ tsp

- Put all ingredients into a food processor and process until well-blended.
- Place in terrine or loaf tin.
- Bake at 180°C 1 hour or until well done.
- Drain excess pan juices.
- Refrigerate for at least two hours. Slice and serve with crusty bread or crackers.

Oxtail Brawn

An excellent dish to serve at a party alongside Windermere Crackers (page 148) on a Dales cheese plate or as part of a charcuterie board.

- Oxtail - 1 washed, dried and cut into joints
- Butter - 60g
- Onion - 1 peeled and quartered
- Mace - a pinch
- Rosemary - 1 sprig
- Parsley - 3 sprigs
- Thyme - 1 sprig
- Small sage leaf - 1
- Bay leaf - 1
- Salt and black pepper
- Malt vinegar - 2 tbs

- Lightly dust the oxtail pieces with seasoned flour. Melt the butter in a saucepan and fry the oxtail until browned all over. Add the onion, herbs, seasoning and vinegar.
- Add cold water to just cover.
- Bring to boil, cover, and simmer until the meat leaves the bones.
- Cool then chop the meat, reserving both the bones and the liquid, but discarding the herbs and a couple of tablespoonfuls of

the onion, also chopped. Butter a terrine or bowl and fill with the meat mixed with the onion.
- Boil the liquid with the bones until it has reduced by half. Strain into the meat the place terrine into the refrigerator to set. Turn out when completely cold.

Black Pudding

This is a recipe for black pudding from the east side of the Pennines, which differs from the north-west version by using pearl barley instead of flair fat to get the white speckles, and Sunderland Spice (page 164) (similar to quatre épices) rather than dried mint.

- Pig's blood - 1 litre
- Cooked pearl barley - 250g
- Rolled oats - 125g
- Fresh breadcrumbs - 500g
- Salt - 2 tbs
- Ground black pepper - 1 tbs
- Whole milk - 360ml
- Fresh parsley - 1 tbs chopped
- Sunderland Spice - 2 tsp (page 164)

- Mix all well and pour into loaf pan(s) lined with plastic wrap, cover with foil.
- Bake in a water bath for 1½ hours at 175°C.
- Cool, slice and fry in a little butter until crisp on both sides.

You can freeze or vacuum seal if not using within three days.

White Pudding

Not seen in the Northern Counties so much as it is across the border in Scotland and over the sea in Ireland, but it was once very popular especially in farming communities.

- Lean pork - 1½ kg boneless, cut into 30cm chunks
- Onions - 1kg chopped coarse
- Bay leaf - 1 medium, crumbled
- Back peppercorns - 6 whole   *(continued over page)*

- Salt - 1 tsp + 4 tsp
- Parsley - 50g chopped coarse
- Green onions - 85g sliced fine
- Garlic - 1 tbs chopped fine
- Cooked white rice - ½ litre
- Dried sage - 1 tbs
- Black pepper - ½ tsp fresh-ground
- Sausage casing - 3 x 1-metre lengths

- Put the pork into a large pan and add enough water to cover it. Bring to a boil over high heat and skim off any foam that rises to the surface. Add the half the onion, bay leaf, peppercorns and 1 teaspoon of salt.
- Reduce heat to low and simmer, partially covered, for 1½ hours. Drain and transfer the pork to a plate.
- When cool, put the pork, remaining onion, parsley, green onions and garlic through the medium blade of a food grinder and place the mixture in a deep bowl. Add the rice, sage and black pepper and 4 teaspoons of salt. Mix everything vigorously by hand until it becomes sticky. Fry a little and check the taste. Adjust the seasoning if needed.
- Stuff sausage into casings and prick in a half-dozen places. You can cook the white pudding in water on a low simmer for 10 minutes before frying in butter. Turn the pudding midway, cook until brown on both sides and cooked through.

Cramlington Dry Sausage

The only dry sausage I have found anywhere in the UK. It was made in farmhouses in November and hung to dry in a breezy outbuilding as flies etc. are gone by that time of year, but also the weather is cooler and the sausage dries more slowly and evenly. When the weather is warm the outside dries more quickly than the inside and prevents the sausage losing moisture, which can lead to the inside being mushy or not curing at all.

- Pork shoulder - 1.5kg coarse minced
- Prague cure No.2 - ¼ tsp (see page V)
- Dry elderberry wine - 110ml

- Garlic paste - 20g
- Sunderland Spice - 4g
- Black pepper - 2g fresh ground
- Salt - 30g
- Yellow mustard seeds - ½ tbs
- Whole black peppercorns - ½ tbs

- Mix the ingredients and stuff into wide casings. Hang up to dry overnight at room temperature.
- Next day weigh each one and make a note of its weight.
- Move to draught-free place at 13°C with 60% humidity, (a modern fridge works well) hang for about a month, or until the sausages have lost ⅔ of their weight.

Summerhouse Spicy Sausage

This gets its name from the village in south Durham where it was served at a local pub alongside mashed potatoes and green beans—it has an unforgettable bite to it. A request for the recipe was politely declined so I bought an extra one, took it home and spent some time analyzing its constitution. I think this is pretty close! This is the basis of Summerhouse Hash (page 197)

- Minced pork - 4kg
- Onions - 4 large grated
- Garlic cloves - 4 minced
- Salt - 3 tbs
- Freshly ground black pepper - 1½ tbs
- Cayenne - 2tbs
- Dried chilli pepper - 1½ tbs crushed
- Ground allspice - 1 tbs
- Fresh parsley - 1 tbs chopped fine
- Fresh thyme - ½ tbs chopped fine
- Ground bay leaf - 1 tsp

- Combine all, mix well & stuff into natural casings.

Shrove bacon

The day before Lent begins is Shrove Tuesday, when households in the Northern Counties used up all the food they would be forbidden during the 40-day meatless fast required by the Church. The traditional pancakes were sometimes accompanied by this bacon, made all the more special with the addition of a sweet and spicy rub. This recipe comes from a Farmer's Weekly collection for 1956 and is attributed to Mrs. Airton of Melsonby, North Yorkshire.

- Thick-cut streaky bacon - 500g
- Brown sugar - 5 tbs
- Cayenne pepper - 1 tsp
- Black pepper - 1 tsp

- Pre-heat oven to 175°C.
- Mix the sugar and spices thoroughly in a bowl.
- Rub each bacon strip with mixture and lay them on a baking sheet lined with foil.
- Bake 15-20 minutes or until crispy, turning the slices half way through.

POTTED MEATS

Meat paste can be made with any leftover meat, or poultry or game, you really shouldn't buy meat and cook it just for potting. The process is essentially the same. In times past, meat and fish pastes were simply cooked leftovers pounded to a paste with a little butter. Nowadays we have the convenience of blenders and food processors that virtually remove the work of making the mixture smooth. We also have access to myriad herbs and spices to lean it in whichever direction our individual fancy takes us.

Meat Paste

You can use lamb, or chicken, or even mince. Pork is particularly good.

- Cooked beef - 350g cut into 1cm cubes
- Butter - 100g softened
- Double cream - 100ml
- Salt, pepper and a pinch of freshly grated nutmeg
- Melted butter, for topping

- Place the beef into a food processor, along with the butter and double cream.
- Season with salt, pepper and nutmeg and process in a blender until you have a fairly smooth paste.
- Wait 10 minutes then check the seasoning before spooning and smoothing into individual ramekins or one larger dish. Wrap the ramekins in film and refrigerate for 30-40 minutes.
- Melt 25-50g of butter and pour over the paste to give a thin coating. Place back in the fridge to set. Keeps 4 or 5 days when refrigerated.

Serve with toast or Sippets (page 11).

Fish Paste

You can use smoked mussels, sardines or any tinned fish for this. Here we use salmon, which is easy to find and inexpensive.

- Cooked red salmon - 350g
- Unsalted butter - 100g softened
- Double cream - 100ml
- Whisky - 1 tsp
- Salt, pepper and a pinch of freshly grated mace
- Melted butter, for topping

- Place the salmon into a food processor, along with the butter, double cream and whisky.
- Season with salt, pepper and mace and process in a blender until you have a smooth paste. For extra smooth, push the paste through a fine sieve.
- Wait 10 minutes then check the seasoning before spooning and smoothing into individual ramekins or one larger dish. Wrap the ramekins in film and refrigerate for 30-40 minutes.
- Melt 25-50g of butter and pour over the paste to give a thin coating. Place back in the fridge to set. Keeps 4 or 5 days when refrigerated.

Serve with toast or Sippets (page 11).

Smoked Fish Paste

The original recipe from Cullercoats calls for bloaters, which is the herring smoked whole, but you can use regular kippers or smoked cod to make this rich and less expensive paste. My favourite is made with smoked trout.

- Smoked fish fillets - 550g skinned
- Butter - 50g softened
- Lemon juice - 2 tbs
- Single cream - 4 tbs
- Ground mace - pinch

- Put the smoked fish, softened butter, lemon juice, cream and mace in a food processor or blender and process until smooth.
- Divide the mixture between four ramekins. Chill for at least an hour. Serve garnished with slices of cucumber and lemon and toast cut into soldiers.

Chicken Liver Paste

This is very smooth and rich—you'll find it in posh restaurants as chicken liver parfait, but I got this recipe from Seaham in County Durham.

- Fresh chicken livers - 250g
- Unsalted butter - 300g
- Garlic - 1 clove chopped fine
- Small shallots - 2 chopped fine
- Fresh thyme - 2 sprigs, leaves only
- Port - 100ml
- Brandy - 50ml
- Double cream - 3 tbs
- Salt & pepper - pinch of each
- Nutmeg - 1/4 tsp

- Melt a knob of the butter in a frying pan. Add the chicken livers and cook for a minute on one side, then turn and cook the other sides for another 1-1½ minutes until they are just brown on the outside but still pink in the middle.

- Transfer the livers and pan juices to a food processor.
- Melt another knob of the butter in the pan, add the garlic, shallots and herbs and fry gently for a few minutes until the shallots have softened but not browned.
- Add the port and brandy and cook 3-4 minutes more then add to the livers in the food processor. Add the thyme leaves, nutmeg, cream, about 1 teaspoon of salt and a good grinding of pepper, and process until smooth.
- Add all but 50g of the remaining butter to the livers and process for another minute or two.
- Push the mixture through a fine sieve and divide between 4 jars or serving pots.
- Melt the remaining 50g of butter and pour over the top of each pot then refrigerate to set the butter. Remove half an hour before you want to eat, to let it soften a little. Serve well chilled with Windermere Crackers (page 148), Sippets (page 11) or toast.

Potted Char

Potted char was a famous Lakeland speciality, very popular once, although it is usually too expensive to have leftovers these days. There are numerous variations and this is a late eighteenth century recipe from Ambleside. This recipe works equally well with fresh trout and salmon.

- Leftover cooked char - about 700g
- Ground spices - 15g mixture of mace and cloves
- White pepper
- Butter - 50g

- Remove all skin and bones from the fish and flake well with a fork.
- Season with spices, salt and pepper.
- Place in 4-6 ramekin dishes and press down well. Melt the butter and spoon melted over the fish until covered well, and place in the refrigerator to set.
- Serve well chilled with Windermere Crackers (page 148), Sippets (page 11) or toast.

Potted Shrimp

The little brown shrimp used for potting are most famously associated with coastal Cumbria. They are a bit of a task to peel, but worth it. Potting is as easy as quickly boiling the peeled shrimp, stuffing a small pot full and covering them in melted butter seasoned with a little mace. Absolutely delicious spread on little soldiers of toasted brown bread. The shrimp also live off the east coast and I remember as a child eating them on Redcar beach in little paper packets —once-a-year-strange and delightfully dry and salty. Not everyone bothered to peel the little shrimp—my dad just threw them one-at-a-time into his mouth, chewed a while then spat out the empty shell.

Seafood Sausage — Serves 4

My own recipe for a very classy dish made with humble ingredients.

- White fish - 250g skinned and boned
- Sea salt - ½ tsp
- Salmon - 125g skinned and boned
- White pepper - ¼ tsp
- Shrimp - 125g peeled
- Egg whites - 2
- Shallots - 2 tbs minced fine
- Flat leaf parsley - 1 bunch chopped

- Cut the fish into small pieces.
- Place ingredients into a food processor and pulse until coarsely chopped. Or, chop finely with a sharp knife and mix thoroughly.
- Roll the mixture into two or three sausages in plastic wrap.
- Poach the sausages in gently simmering water for 5 minutes, drain and let cool.
- Remove wrap when sausages are cool. Cut sausages on the bias into finger-thick slices and serve.

SAVOURY PIES

I could probably live on just pies and I bet I'm not alone there. The savoury pie is the unsung national dish of Britain, with a nod only to those other pretenders chicken tikka masala, fish n' chips and roast beef. Pies get eaten quietly and without praise all the time. They have provided the main component of the workers' meal break in coal mines, factories and fields for centuries. Everybody has a favourite and often a memory to go with it. One of the fondest memories of serving my apprenticeship in a factory in Newton Aycliffe was the break time pies sold in the canteen. They were made a stone's throw away by local baker Jim Whitton and my favourite was the mince and onion. Alas, Jim's Pies closed its doors in 1974 and the recipe on page 112 is as close as I can get to that much missed fare.

Sweet Mutton Pies

A Westmoreland favourite from the 19th century. You don't see much mutton anymore, so these days it's lamb. Housewives would use leftovers for these pies.

- Short crust pastry - 500g
- Slow-braised mutton - 200g cold and diced
- An equal amount, by weight, of apples, peeled and cubed
- Sugar - 3 tbs
- Nutmeg - pinch
- Prunes or raisins - 1 tbs chopped
- Salt & pepper to taste

- Make up the pastry, keeping about a third back for the tops of the pies.
- Roll out and cut circles to fit muffin pans.
- Mix the meat and fruit together seasoning well.
- Fill each pie, adding a grating of nutmeg, sprinkle of sugar and a few dots of butter on top of each.
- Cover with pastry lids cut from the remainder of the pastry and bake at about 230°C for about 30 minutes or until the crust goes a light golden brown.

If you want to serve these pies hot, bake without a slit in the pastry. If you intend to serve them cold, as is more usual, make a slit in the pastry lids before baking, then once out of the oven and still hot, run in heated red currant jelly through the slit. When the pie goes cold the jelly will reset and form a sweet, delicious layer.

Corned Beef Pasties

There are two forms of corned beef: a spice-rubbed, marinated piece of brisket that is cooked slowly, or tinned. The term 'corned beef' comes from the preparation of the meat when it is rubbed with salt grains the size of corn kernels (same as the word peppercorns). This recipe uses the tinned variety.

- Shortcrust pastry - 900g (page 118)
- Vegetable oil - 2 tbs
- Onions - 450g peeled and sliced
- Tinned corned beef 450g cubed

- Tomato ketchup - 2 tbs
- paprika - 1 tsp
- Salt and pepper - to taste
- Egg - 1 beaten for glazing

- Roll out the pastry and cut out 6 circles 20cm in diameter.
- Heat the oil in a frying pan and cook the onions until starting to soften. Remove from heat and cool.
- Stir in the corned beef, paprika and tomato ketchup and season well. Divide the mixture between the six circles and crimp the edges together.
- Brush with a little beaten egg. Place on a baking tray and bake in a 200°C oven for 20-30 minutes until the pastry is golden. Serve hot or cold.

Cockfield Pasties

Ovington Edge and Cockfield Fell
Are the coldest spots between heaven and hell
~ old saying

Well, these pasties have a peppery bite that will keep you warm no matter what the weather.

- Shortcrust pastry - 500g (page 118)
Filling
- Minced beef - 700g
- Minced pork - 700g
- Green onion - 1 chopped
- Onion - 1 medium chopped
- Salt - 1 tsp
- Black pepper -1 tsp
- White pepper - 1 tsp
- Cayenne pepper - 1 tsp or to taste
- Plain flour - 40g *(continued over page)*

- Brown the meat, stirring constantly. Pour off any liquid produced. Add onion, green onion and seasonings. Cook until onions are very soft. Adjust seasoning if needed.
- Sprinkle the flour onto the mixture and stir until well combined.
- Remove from heat and cool to room temperature.
- Cut off a handful of dough about the size of a large egg. Dust lightly with flour, then carefully roll it out into a circle the size of a saucer.
- Place two heaping tablespoons of filling inside the circle. Dampen the edges, fold over, and crimp the edges with a fork or fingers to seal. Poke a few holes in the pastry with a fork. Repeat until all the filling dough is used.
- Place on a baking tray in a pre-heated oven at 175°C for about 15 min, or until golden brown.

Potato Pasties — recipe from Dora Kelly, Alston

"All you do is make a shortcrust dough. Don't worry about keeping your hands out of it, because it works better when it's tougher. My father says that his grandmother made big ones and sliced them up to serve, but my mother always made little ones so we each got our own." - DK

- Shortcrust pastry - 500g (page 118)

- Roll out a thin circles of dough about the size of a saucer, prop up one side on the rolling pin, and fill with the following:

- Potatoes - 1 large sliced really thin
- Minced beef - 250g
- Onion - 1 chopped fine
- Salt and pepper - to taste

- Close the circle, crimp it with a little water and bake in a 175°C oven until the pasty is browned and the contents are cooked. Great hot or cold!

Woodland Mushroom Pie

Although not prolific, wild mushrooms are well worth the trip into the fields and woods of late Summer and Autumn—their earthy flavour cannot be matched by anything farmed. I would love to tell you where to find them but mushroom patches are the secret bailiwick of mushroom pickers. Be careful should you venture out to find them, if you don't know with certainty what you've found— leave it in the ground. Ordinary white button mushrooms mixed with some exotics from the supermarket, such as crimini, shiitake and oyster mushrooms, will still make an excellent pie.

- Wild mushrooms - 600g mixed
- Butter - 3 tbs
- Chicken - 700g diced
- Plain flour - 1 tbs
- Lemon - 1
- Onion - 1 large chopped
- Sour cream - 200ml
- Rough puff pastry - two crusts (page 118)

Preheat oven to 220°C.

- Fry mushrooms in butter until tender and most of the liquid evaporates.
- Add chopped onion, fry until translucent.
- Add chicken, cook until tender.
- Sprinkle in flour, stir, cook for 2 minutes.
- Add lemon juice, stir in.
- Add sour cream, stir well and cool to room temperature.
- Line a 25cm pie pan with flaky pastry.
- Add cooled filling, then add top crust and crimp closed.
- Cut vent hole and brush with egg wash (one egg, 1 tsp water, mixed).
- Place pie on baking sheet in oven, mid-rack.
- Bake 15 minutes, or until top crust begins to brown.
- Lower temperature to 175°C and continue baking for another 30-40 minutes.
- Serve warm or cold with a green salad.

Cumberland Game Pie

- Shortcut pastry - 1.2kg (page 118)

- Vegetable oil - 2 tbs
- Large onions - 2 peeled and diced
- White mushrooms - 120g sliced
- Back bacon - 120g diced
- Game meat - 1kg (venison, rabbit, pigeon, etc.), boned and diced
- Orange - 1 zest & juice only
- Port wine - 70ml
- Chicken stock - 300ml
- Redcurrant jelly - 1 tbs
- Bay leaves - 4
- Plain flour - 30g
- Egg for glazing - 1

- Brown the game, set aside.
- Fry the onions until soft and translucent. Add the bacon and mushrooms and cook for 5 minutes.
- Sprinkle in the flour and cook for 2 minutes. Season well, add bay leaves, orange juice and zest, redcurrant jelly, stock & port.
- Bring to the boil, add the game and simmer gently for 1 hour or until the meat is tender. Allow to cool.
- Flour the inside of a 33cm pie pan. Roll out pastry base & press into the pan, leaving an overhang of 1cm. Fill with the game mixture. Roll out and add pastry lid, wet and crimp with a fork. Cut a steam hole in the middle and glaze with beaten egg.
- Bake for 30 minutes on bottom shelf of a 190°C oven, followed by 30 minutes on top shelf until the pastry is golden brown.

Serve with creamy mash, steamed cabbage and gravy.

Pheasant Pie

- Pheasant - 1 boiled and deboned
- Plain flour - 2 tbs
- Onions - 1 chopped
- Celery - ½ stalk, chopped
- Salt and pepper - 1 tsp each
- Eggs - 2 hard boiled and sliced
- Broth from cooked pheasant - 450ml

- Cut up the pheasant and put in a plastic bag with the flour, onions, celery, and salt. Shake until everything is well coated. Place into a large pie dish.
- Slice eggs over this mixture and season with pepper.
- Carefully pour in the broth over mixture, let stand a few minutes before putting on crust.

Pie crust:
- Butter or margarine - 4 tbs melted.
- Buttermilk or plain milk - 250ml
- Self raising flour - 125g
- Salt - ½ tsp

- Beat together to form a smooth batter, then spread on top of pie.
- Bake at 180°C for 30 minutes or until crust has browned and pie is bubbly.

Blue Wensleydale Flan

As fancy and as rustic as anything you can find anywhere. Blue mold is, I think, a relatively new addition of this ancient cheese. You can substitute any blue cheese, or if you are adventurous, make your own Eldon Blue (page 194). The original recipe called for Wensleydale cheese, but of course Blue Weardale is excellent too.

- Shortcrust pastry - 300g (page 118)
- Vegetable oil - 2tbs
- Butter - 25g

(continued over page)

- Onions - 350g sliced fine
- Leeks - 675g sliced
- Garlic - 2 cloves crushed or chopped fine
- Fresh thyme - 2 tsp leaves only
- Caster sugar - 1 tsp
- Plain flour - 1 tbs
- Eggs - 3
- Double cream - 250ml
- Blue Wensleydale cheese - 100g crumbled
- Fresh grated parmesan - 2 tbs
- Seasoning to taste

- Line a 25cm flan tin or dish with the pastry. Place in the refrigerator to chill.
- Heat the oil and the butter in a pan until melted. Add the onions, leeks, sugar, garlic and thyme and cook gently until they have started to turn golden brown and are soft. Allow to cool slightly. Fold in the flour and add seasoning.
- Beat the eggs and cream together and add to the onion mix. Fold in half the parmesan and all the blue cheese.
- Spoon the mixture into the flan case and sprinkle with the remaining parmesan.
- Bake in a pre-heated 190°C oven or about 50 minutes until golden brown and set.

Leek Flan

Another great way to use leeks after the annual leek show. This one came with Welsh coal mining families who moved north during the late 1800s.

- Shortcrust pastry - (page 118)

- Smoked streaky bacon - 225g chopped
- Leeks - 450g cleaned and sliced
- Dales cheese - 100g crumbled
- Eggs - 3
- Milk - 225ml
- Freshly ground black pepper

- Fry the bacon pieces until browned, remove and add the leeks to the frying pan. Cook until soft. Place the bacon, leeks and cheese in the flan case.
- Beat the eggs and add the milk, season and pour over the bacon, leeks and cheese. Bake at 180°C for 25 minutes until just set.
- Roll out the pastry and line a 28 x 20cm flan tin. Bake blind at 200°C for 10 minutes.

Serve hot or cold.

Cheviot Pie

Originating in the England/Scotland border country where the quality of meat is always excellent, this is a one-crust suet pie which makes a small amount of meat go a long way. North of the border it is known as Teviot pie.

- Lean minced beef - 450g
- Onion - 1 medium, chopped
- Beef stock - 250ml
- Yorkshire Relish (page 164) - 2 tsp
- Plain flour - 225g
- Cornflour - 25g (1 tbs)
- Baking powder - 1 tsp
- Shredded suet - 75g
- Milk - 250ml

Pre-heat oven to 180°C

- Put the meat in a large saucepan and cook over a medium heat in its own fat until it starts to brown. Add the onion and cook for a further 5 minutes until softened.
- Add the stock and Yorkshire Relish. Simmer for 15-20 minutes.
- Put the flour, cornflour and suet in a bowl, then gradually stir in the milk to form a thick batter.
- Put the meat in a 1 litre pie dish. Cover with the batter and bake for 30-35 minutes until risen and browned.

Minced Beef Pie — Makes 6 pies

- Shortcrust pastry - 1kg (page 118)

- Minced beef - 550-600g
- Onion - 1 minced
- Butter - 2 tbs
- Allspice - ½ tsp
- Salt - 2 tsp
- White pepper - ¼ tsp
- Beef stock - 350ml

- Melt butter in a medium frying pan over a medium heat. Add onion and cook for 2 minutes, stirring often.
- Add minced beef, salt, pepper and allspice. When meat is brown, add flour and stir well. Then add the stock, stir well until mixture thickens and simmer for 30 minutes, stirring often.
- Remove pan from heat and refrigerate for one hour.
- Line six 150mm pie pans with pie crusts.
- Spoon minced meat evenly into each pie.
- Brush crust edge with egg mixture. Roll out top crusts and fit loosely over filling, crimping edges together with a fork.
- Brush crust with egg mixture and make vent holes with a fork.
- Bake at 220°C for 10 minutes. Reduce heat to 175°C and bake for 40 minutes or until the pies are golden. Remove from oven and allow 5 minutes to cool before serving.

Chicken and Leek and Pasties

A classic combination in a handy form originating in mining villages of Northumberland and Durham. I got this recipe over the phone from a lady in Morpeth who consulted her friend as we spoke: "Bella ... hoo lang de ye cyuk a leek n' chicken pasty?"

- Rough puff pastry (page 118)

- Butter - 2 tbs
- Leeks - 2 or 3 (about 450g), washed and sliced fine
- Fresh thyme - 1 tsp chopped

- Heavy cream - 160ml
- English mustard - 1 tsp
- Sea salt and freshly ground black pepper
- Leftover cooked chicken - 350g sliced thick
- Egg - 1 beaten with 1 tbs milk, for glazing.

- Melt the butter in a frying pan, add the leeks and thyme, and cook gently for 5 to 10 minutes, until the leeks are very tender.
- Stir in cream and simmer 5 minutes to reduce and thicken. Stir in mustard and cooked chicken, season well, and let cool.

Preheat the oven to 190°C.

- Roll out pastry to about 3mm thick. Using a plate or a cake pan as a template, cut out three 20cm circles. Re-roll the trimmings to get a fourth circle.
- Spoon the mixture onto one half of each circle. Brush the pastry edges with a little water, fold the other half of the pastry over the filling to form a half-moon, and crimp well to seal.
- Place on a lightly oiled baking sheet and brush the tops with egg wash. Bake for 25 minutes, until golden brown. Eat hot or cold.

Creamy Sage and Onion Flan

Another way to rejoice in the glory of sage and onion stuffing! I know people who would happily forgo everything served at Christmas dinner so long as they got stuffing and gravy. Sage and onion are not only a good combination for stuffings but are also very good together in this flan.

- Shortcrust pastry - (page 118)

- Butter - 90g
- Onions - 2 sliced
- Plain flour - 150g
- Water - 2-3 tbs
- Curd or cottage cheese - 110g
- Milk - 150ml
- Eggs - 2 beaten
- Fresh sage - 1 tbs chopped

- Melt 25g of the butter and fry the onions until soft.
- Blend the curd cheese, milk and egg. Beat in the sage with a fork.
- Roll out pastry and line a 15cm flan tin.
- Drain the onions, spread them over the pastry case and pour the liquid mixture over the onions.
- Bake at 200°C for 40 minutes until set and golden.

Rabbit Pie

Rabbit dishes used to appear regularly on the tables of the Northern Counties before the 1960s—rabbit was plentiful and almost free. The introduction of myxomatosis disease to kill the surplus population put an end to that though. Wild rabbits are best for this pie, but you can use farm-raised too.

- Shortcrust pastry (page 118)

- Rabbit - 450g skinned, boned and cubed
- Streaky bacon - 110g rinded and chopped
- Potatoes - 2 sliced
- Leek - 1 sliced
- Fresh parsley - 1 tbs chopped
- Dried mixed herbs - ¼ tsp
- Chicken stock
- Egg - 1 beaten

Pre-heat oven to 190°C.

- Fill a 2 litre pie dish with alternate layers of rabbit, bacon and vegetables, sprinkling with the herbs. Half fill with stock.
- Roll out the pastry on a lightly floured surface to 5cm wider than the top of the dish. Cut a 2.5cm strip from the outer edge and line the dampened rim of the dish. Dampen the pastry rim and cover with the pastry lid. Trim and seal the edges. Make a hole in the centre to let the steam escape.
- Decorate with pastry leaves and brush with egg. Bake for 30 minutes. Cover loosely with foil. Reduce to 180°C for a further hour. Serve hot.

Yorkshire Growler

Growler is the name of the pork pie when it's really big ... a kilo or more of meat filling. They come in two other sizes—small or individual, and tiny or party size. You can shape the growler into an oblong loaf pan and cut into slices, or keep it in the traditional round shape and serve it in wedges. It is has three elements: the hot-water crust, the pork filling and the jelly (not optional).

- Hot water pastry crust (page 119)

Filling:
*I personally add a little Cure No. 1 (see page V) to my filling to keep the pork pink, but you can partially achieve this by substituting a third of the pork with minced bacon or ham. If you don't do either, the meat will be a less appetizing grey-brown colour, but still tasty.

- Pork shoulder - 1kg diced small or coarse-minced
- Dried sage - 2 tsp
- Salt - 2 tsp
- White pepper - 2 tsp

Jelly
Pig trotters make the best pork pie jelly, but gelatine is a quicker, simpler option - just follow the instructions on the packet.

- Pig trotter - 1 cleaned
- Water - 1 litre
- Onion - 1 sliced
- Salt - 1 tsp
- White pepper - 1 tsp

- Place the trotter in a saucepan with water, onion, salt and pepper. Bring to the boil and simmer for 4 hours. Strain and keep aside.

Build and bake:
A growler can be hand-raised, but I find it better to use a round cake pan or an oblong loaf pan. Keeping aside a third of the pastry for the lid, mold the rest into the pan leaving a lip overhanging the rim.

- Mix together the pork, sage, salt and pepper. Carefully fill the pie with the mixture, pressing the mixture down at the edges to leave a dome in the centre.
- Flatten or roll the remaining pastry into a circle for the lid.
- Brush the top edge of the pie base with beaten egg, press on the lid and seal the edges of the lid and body with a fork or by crimping.
- Cut a round hole in the centre of the lid. This is where the jelly stock will be added when the pie is baked.
- Bake the growler in the preheated 180°C oven for 20 minutes.
- Reduce the temperature to 160°C and cook a further 50 minutes.
- Halfway through the cooking time, remove pie from the oven and brush with egg wash. Return to the oven to finish cooking.
- Remove from the oven and allow to cool. After one hour place in the fridge until cold.

Filling the Pies with Jellied Stock:

- Gently insert the tip of a funnel into the hole in the lid.
- Reheat stock and pour carefully into the hole in the top of the pie a little at a time to seep down into all the gaps and crevices.
- When the pie is full of stock, return to the fridge until the jelly has set, preferably overnight.

DESSERTS

Dessert—variously known around the Northern Counties as pudding, duff, afters or simply sweet, is a much loved part of any meal. A dessert course is reserved for special occasions in the home, although when dining out it's often the reason people went to the restaurant. Ours are all traditional treats that were served at home on Sundays or birthdays or for other celebrations.

Basics: How to Make Pastry

Note: Bicarbonate of soda (bicarb) and baking powder are not the same thing—baking powder has a small amount of cream of tartar and sometimes cornflour in it. In recipes that call for baking powder, you may substitute weight-for-weight self-raising flour for plain flour and omit the bicarb and baking powder if you wish.

Shortcrust Pastry

This pastry is used for sweet and savoury flans, pies, tarts, tartlets, pastries, etc. If the recipe calls for 'sweet shortcrust' specifically, simply add 2 tbs of caster sugar to the dry ingredients.

- Plain flour - 450g
- Salt - $\frac{1}{4}$ tsp
- Butter - 100g
- Lard - 100g
- Cold water - to mix

- Sift the flour and salt into a bowl.
- Add the fats. Cut into the flour with a knife then rub in with your fingertips. The mixture should resemble fine breadcrumbs.
- Sprinkle water over the crumbs. Mix to a stiff crumbly-looking paste with a round-ended knife. Draw together with fingertips, turn out on to a lightly floured work surface. Knead quickly until smooth and crack free.
- Wrap in plastic film and set to rest in the fridge for 20 minutes.
- Roll out and use as required. If not to be used immediately, transfer to a polythene bag or wrap in aluminium foil and freeze.

Rough Puff Pastry

Not so light as flaky or puff pastry but way easier to make and gives you a nice crispy crust. Good for both sweet and savoury pies, pasties and sausage rolls.

- Plain flour - 253g
- Pinch of salt
- Lard or hard vegetable fat - 85g

- Butter or margarine - 85g
- Lemon juice - 1tsp
- Cold water - to mix

- Sieve the flour and salt into a bowl and add the fat, cut into lumps about the size of a walnut. Stir into the flour.
- Add the lemon juice and enough cold water to make stiff dough.
- Turn on to a lightly floured board and roll out into an oblong.
- Fold one end up, leaving about one-third of the strip to fold down, seal the edges with the rolling pin and give the pastry a half turn.
- Repeat until the pastry has been rolled and folded four times.
- Refrigerate for 20 minutes before using.

Puff Pastry

If you want a fully puff pastry, simply make the recipe for rough puff pastry (above) but butter the entire surface of the pastry after you have rolled it out once, then continue as for rough puff, but roll and fold it at least 7 times, refrigerating for 10 minutes between each roll.

Hot-Water Crust Pastry

For all pork pies, growlers etc. this pastry is resistant to moisture and stays crisp.

- Lard - 110g
- Water - 280ml
- Plain flour - 500g
- Salt - 2 tsp

- Put the lard and water into a saucepan and bring to the boil.
- Sieve the flour into a large bowl with the salt.
- Make a well in the middle of the flour and pour in the lard and water mixture.
- Mix thoroughly to form a dough (use a wooden spoon, it will be quite hot!)
- Cover the dough with plastic wrap and let it rest rest 20 minutes.
- Roll out to a thickness of 3mm and mold into pie pan by hand.

Suet Pastry

An old-fashioned pastry used for steamed puddings both sweet and savoury, roly-poly puddings and dumplings.

- Plain flour - 225g
- Baking powder - 1 tsp
- Salt - ½ tsp
- Shredded suet - 112g
- Cold water

- Sieve the flour, baking powder and salt together in a bowl.
- Add the shredded suet and mix well.
- Mix to a stiff dough with the water.

Summer Pudding

Berries grow well in the Northern Counties. Raspberries seem to thrive in the cooler conditions of the north and often feature in gardens, whereas blackberries are still gleaned from hedgerows and wasteland by armies of kids in the late Summer and early Autumn. If berries are in short supply you can bulk up the filling with a diced dessert apple.

- Mixed Summer fruit (such as raspberries, strawberries, fresh currants, blackberries, blueberries, etc.)
- Caster sugar - 185g
- Blackcurrant cordial or cassis - 120ml
- White bread - 1 medium loaf slightly stale

- Pudding basin - 1 litre

- Put the fruit into a pan, pour the sugar over the fruit and stir gently to mix together.
- Place the pan over a medium heat and bring gently to the boil.
- When the juices begin to flow, raise the heat slightly and simmer for about 2-3 minutes. Then turn off the heat and stir in the cassis or blackcurrant cordial.

- Remove the crusts from the bread, cut into triangles and line a buttered 1 litre pudding basin so there are no gaps.
- Spoon all of the fruit and juices into the pudding basin. Cover the top of the fruit with more wedges of bread. Place the pudding basin on a plate to collect any juices.
- Place a saucer that fits neatly inside the bowl on top to cover the upper layer of bread, then weigh the saucer down (tinned goods work well). Let the pudding cool, then place in fridge overnight.
- The next day, remove the weight and the saucer. Run a thin blade around the edges, then invert the basin onto a shallow serving plate.
- Turn the pudding out, cut in wedges and serve with thick cream.

Wowie Dumplings

My mother named these—she may even have invented them—and while I think the name is well-suited, they're so delicious they must be bad for your health.

- Self-raising flour 120g
- Butter - 3tbs
- Egg - 1 large
- Milk - 1 tbs

- Rub the butter into the flour until the mixture is fine and crumbly, and make a well in the middle.
- Combine egg and milk and fork gently into the flour mixture to form a soft dough.

- Water - 250ml
- Sugar - 200g
- Butter - 3 tbs
- Golden syrup - 2 tbs
- Lemon juice - 60ml

- Place the water in a large pan with the sugar, butter, golden syrup and lemon juice. Stir over medium heat until combined and the sugar has dissolved.

(continued over page)

- Bring syrup to a boil, then gently drop tablespoons of dumpling dough into the syrup. Cover and reduce the heat to a simmer.
- Cook for 20 minutes and test for doneness—a knife inserted into a dumpling should come out clean. Spoon out the dumplings and drizzle with the syrup.
- Serve the warm dumplings immediately with ice cream.

Banana Loaf

One of my passions is collecting bits of folklore, and I was once told this story about the first banana that came into County Durham after the fruit had been long absent on account of the Second World War. A soldier returning home from overseas had stuffed a hand of bananas into his kitbag and was suddenly hungry on the train ride from Darlington to Bishop Auckland. In peeling the banana he drew curious looks from two little girls sitting opposite. "Have you never seen a banana?" said the soldier. The little girls shook their heads, so he broke off a piece and offered it to them. One reached over, took the fruit, and bit into it just as the train entered the blackness of Shildon tunnel. When they emerged two miles and several minutes later, she looked at her sister and said, "Don't eat it ... they make you blind."

Preheat oven to 175°C. Butter and flour 25cm x15cm loaf pan.

- Plain flour - 220g
- Baking soda - 1 tsp
- Baking powder - 1 tsp
- Salt - ½ tsp
- Butter - 110g softened
- White sugar - 150g
- Large eggs - 2
- Very ripe bananas - 230g (2-3 large bananas) mashed
- Fresh lemon juice - 2 tbs
- Vanilla extract - 1½ tsp

- In a medium bowl, whisk together the flour, baking soda, baking powder and salt.
- Beat the butter and sugar until light and fluffy.
- Add the eggs one at a time, beating well after each addition.
- Add the mashed bananas, lemon juice and vanilla extract and mix well.
- Add the flour mixture and beat until just incorporated. Do not over mix. Pour the batter into the prepared loaf pan and bake until a tester inserted into the centre comes out clean, 40-45 minutes.
- Let cool in the pan for about 10 minutes, then turn out onto a wire rack to cool completely.

Peaches and Cream

If you think the Northern Counties is no place to grow fruit other than the indigenous bounty of the hedgerow, think again. In the mid-1800s at Stanwick Hall near Aldborough St. John in North Yorkshire, gardener William Higgie had a conservatory where he grew palms, bananas and orchids, while in the fruit houses grew peaches, grapes, figs and nectarines. The once famous Stanwick nectarine was described in the 1884 edition of Hogg's Fruit Manual: "Fruit: large, roundish oval. Skin: lively green where shaded and purplish red where exposed to sun. Flesh: white, melting, rich, sugary and delicious. Kernel: sweet like that of a sweet almond." The Stanwick nectarine was developed from Syrian peach stones, brought home by Lady Prudhoe—later to become Duchess of Northumberland—and planted at Stanwick in March 1843. The buds were grafted onto a Bellegarde Peach and the resulting nectarine first fruited in 1846. Country Life described it as "the largest and finest in flavour then known." William and his wife, Jane Turnbull, from Alnwick, and their eight children lived in a tied cottage on the estate until he retired and went to live in Gilling West.

It's tempting to try to devise a peach pie or otherwise cooked dessert using nectarines and peaches, but the truth is you can't improve on fresh peaches or

nectarines served with double cream, whipped cream, or ice cream. When they're in season I'd recommend you do just that. If you can only get tinned fruit, why not do as my mother did and make whimsical peach eggs:

- Cover one large oatmeal biscuit (page 146) completely with whipped cream, then place a peach half on top so it looks like a fried egg. Nectarines or apricots work just as well.

Rough Strawberry and Rhubarb Pie

A really easy to make pie from the Cleveland area that is very forgiving of rough handling, hence the name.

- Puff-pastry - 397g (page 118)

- White sugar - 125g
- Cornflour - 45g
- Fresh strawberries - 150g hulled and quartered
- Fresh rhubarb - 300g sliced

Preheat oven to 240°C

- Line a baking sheet with parchment paper or foil. Dust the pastry and rolling pin lightly with flour. Roll pastry into a thin circle, about 35-40cm wide. Edges should be uneven. Lift pastry onto baking sheet; don't worry if some pastry overhangs edge.
- In a large bowl, stir 125ml sugar with 3 tbs cornflour until blended. If using frozen rhubarb, stir in an additional tablespoon. Add strawberries to cornflour mixture. Slice rhubarb into 1cm pieces and toss with strawberries.
- Turn fruit mixture into centre of pastry, forming a high dome and leaving a pastry edge that is at least 8cm wide. Fold pastry over fruit, overlapping edges as needed. Pie will flatten slightly as it bakes. Centre of pie should not be covered with pastry and edges should be uneven. Brush pastry very lightly with water, then sprinkle with 1 tbs sugar.
- Place on bottom rack of oven. Immediately reduce oven temperature to 190°C and bake until fruit bubbles and pastry is

golden, from 40 to 45 minutes. To prevent fruit from drying out on top, during last 15 minutes of baking, cover fruit only with a small circle of foil. Let pie stand for 5 minutes before serving. Cut into wedges and serve with vanilla ice cream or lightly sweetened whipped cream. Pie is best warm.

Bramble Cobble

In other parts of the country this is called a cobbler. The name seems to come from the similarity of the dumplings to cobblestones. Wild blueberries are difficult to find, although they do grow in the Northern Counties, but with luck the garden will give up lots of raspberries and, of course, there are always lots of blackberries in the hedgerow waiting for your attention. Pick them and freeze them for times of the year they are not available fresh.

- Apples - 1kg peeled, cored and sliced
- White sugar - 100g
- Butter - 1 tbs
- Blackberries, raspberries, or blueberries or a mixture - 500g

- Put the apples into a saucepan with the sugar, butter and a couple of tablespoons of water.
- Heat very gently until the juices begin to run.
- Very gentle simmer for about 15 minutes, stirring occasionally.
- Taste for sweetness and add more sugar if you like, but keep it on the tart side.
- Stir in the blackberries and pile the mixture into a pie dish or other ovenproof dish, leaving a good couple of centimetres spare at the top.

Cobbles:
- Milk - 100ml warmed
- Lemon juice - 1 tsp
- Plain flour - 100g
- Baking powder - 1 tbs
- Butter - 75g
- Ground almonds - 100g
- Caster sugar - 50g

(continued over page)

- Mix the warm milk with the lemon juice and set aside.
- Sift the flour and baking powder into a bowl and rub in the butter until you have fine crumbs.
- Stir in the ground almonds and sugar, then mix in the milk to give a soft dough. You can do all this in a food processor, pulsing first the flour, baking powder and butter, then the almonds and sugar, then the milk.
- Drop each cobble—not quite touching the one next to it—over the fruit in the dish. There should be 6 or 8.
- Place the dish in the centre of a moderate oven 180°C and bake for about 30 minutes, until the cobbles are puffed and golden, like crusty scones.
- Leave to cool for 15 minutes or so then serve.

Gurney Valley Cheesecake (an easy no-bake recipe)

I have made dozens of cheesecakes over the years—all baked. When I was given this recipe (so simple it was hastily scribbled on a bit of paper in a pub near Bishop Auckland) I had my doubts, but now it's the only one I make.

Crust:
- Ginger snaps or digestive biscuits - 145g finely crushed
- Butter - 45g
- White sugar - 40g
- In a bowl, mix together crushed biscuits with melted butter and the sugar.
- Press into a 20cm spring-form pan. Place in refrigerator until ready for use.

Filling:
- Cream cheese - 450g
- White sugar - 65g
- Lemon juice - 30ml
- Heavy cream - 120ml whipped
- Fresh strawberries - sliced

- In a bowl, beat together cream cheese, sugar and lemon juice.

- In another bowl, whip the cream, then fold it into the cream cheese mixture.
- Spread onto the biscuit base in the pan.
- Freeze for 1 hour, covered with foil.
- Top with sliced strawberries.
- Place in fridge for 30 minutes, remove from pan, slice and serve.

Lindisfarne Syllabub

Syllabub is a very old dessert and is fairly simple to whip up. This version incorporates Lindisfarne mead. If you can't get it, substitute sweet white wine.

- Milk - 150ml
- Soft brown sugar - 90g
- Vanilla essence - ½ tsp
- Lindisfarne mead or sweet white wine - 150ml
- Extra thick double cream - 600ml
- Mace - a touch, ground

- Chill all the ingredients and prepare shortly before serving.
- Mix everything together except the cream and the mace in a punch bowl.
- Beat the cream lightly and add to the other ingredients.
- Sprinkle with ground mace before serving.

Newcastle Pudding

A steamed lemon-flavoured bread pudding from the regional capital.

- Milk - 450ml
- Lemon - 1 zest only
- Eggs - 3 beaten
- Sugar - 50g
- White bread - 6 slices, thickly buttered with crusts removed

Sauce:
- Caster sugar - 50g
- Water - 600ml
- Lemon - 1 zest and juice

(continued over page)

- Eggs - 2 beaten
- Butter - 75g

- Warm the milk in a pan and stir in the lemon zest. Cover and leave to infuse for 1 hour.
- Beat the eggs and sugar well together, then pour into the milk and mix well.
- Line a well-buttered 900ml - 1.2 litre pudding basin with the slices of bread, buttered side inwards.
- Pour the milk mixture over the bread and let soak for 1 hour.
- Cover with buttered greaseproof paper and kitchen foil and tie down.
- Place the pudding basin in a saucepan of boiling water, and steam for 40-45 minutes, topping up the water as necessary.
- Make the sauce by boiling the sugar, water and lemon zest and juice together in a saucepan until slightly reduced and thickened.
- Pour into a double saucepan or a bowl in a pan filled with boiling water and stir in the beaten eggs and butter.
- Bring back to the boil and whisk continuously until the sauce thickens.
- Strain into a warm jug or sauceboat and serve hot.
- Turn out the pudding on to a warm serving dish and serve with the lemon sauce.

Mucky-mouth Pie

So-called because they stain your mouth, these originated in moorland areas where bilberries grow well. A bakery stall at Catterick market was where this recipe came from, ready printed and free with the purchase of a pie. Blueberries, larger and easier to get than bilberries, make a good substitute.

- Sweet shortcrust pastry - 340g (page 118)
- Cooking apples - 2 large peeled, cored and sliced
- Bilberries - 450g
- Fresh mint - 2 tbs chopped fine
- Caster sugar - 110g
- Icing sugar - 45g
- Egg white - 1

Preheat oven to 200°C

- Roll out half the pastry and line a greased 25cm pie dish. Chill.
- Mix the apple with the bilberries and mint.
- Pour into the pie base and sprinkle with sugar.
- Roll out the rest of the pastry to make a lid and bake for 30 minutes. Turn the heat down to 170°C.
- Whisk egg white until stiff, then whisk in the icing sugar until you have peaks. Spread over the pie and return to oven for about 10 minutes until lightly browned.

Sly Cakes—Makes a dozen

There is all manner of conjecture as to why they're called sly cakes ... but nothing I have found convincing.

• Shortcrust pastry - 500g (page 118)

Filling:
• Dried figs - 225g chopped
• Walnut pieces - 75g chopped
• Currants - 50g
• Raisins - 50g
• Fresh milk, to glaze

- Put the figs, walnuts, currants and raisins into a saucepan with 150ml water and cook, uncovered, stirring continuously, until the water has evaporated and the fruit mixture is soft and thick. Leave to cool.
- Divide the dough into two, and roll out one half to fit a shallow 18 x 28cm tin. Spread the fruit mixture over the dough, then roll out the remaining dough and use to cover the filling. Seal the edges well and mark into 12 squares. Brush the top with a little milk to glaze.
- Bake at 190°C for about 40 minutes, until golden brown. Leave to cool, then cut into the marked squares.

Soul Cakes

Soul cakes were once the 'treat' given out to Northern Counties children who turned up at the door at Halloween. In coal mining areas, kids held up a home-made lantern fashioned of a candle in a tin and called out, "Jack shine thee Maggie!" which was meant to mimic the call of a coal miner asking a comrade to hold up a magnesium lamp. You never see soul cakes anymore, but in case you feel you need to revive the tradition, here is the recipe.

Preheat oven to 180°C

- Butter - 240g
- Castor sugar -100g
- Eggs, - 2 lightly beaten
- Malt vinegar - 2 tsp
- Plain flour - 400g sifted
- Nutmeg - ¼ tsp
- Cinnamon, ginger, allspice - 1 tsp each

- Cream butter and sugar.
- Mix in eggs and add vinegar.
- Add sifted flour and spices and mix to a stiff dough.
- Knead thoroughly, roll out 6mm thick, cut into 75mm rounds and set on greased baking sheets.
- Prick cakes with a fork and bake about 25 minutes.

North Country Tart

A beautiful tart combining raspberry preserve and a syrupy mixture of egg and coconut. Great hot or cold.

- Shortcrust pastry - 225g (page 118)

- Fresh raspberry conserve - 200ml (see below)
- Butter - 50g
- Caster sugar - 25g
- Golden syrup - 25g
- Desiccated coconut - 110g
- Small egg - 1 beaten

Fresh raspberry conserve:
- Place fresh raspberries over low heat with their equal weight in sugar. Stir gently until the sugar is completely melted, then remove from heat and set aside.

Preheat oven to 190°C

- Roll out the pastry on a lightly floured surface until large enough to line a 20cm pie plate, trim the edge.
- Cover pastry with the raspberry conserve.
- Melt the butter, golden syrup and caster sugar together in a saucepan over a low heat, then stir in the coconut and egg. Combine well and spread on top of the raspberry conserve.
- Bake for 25-30 minutes.

Bishop Auckland Cheese-cakes
"These were a bite that melted in the mouth and the recipe was rarely given away." - Peggy Hutchinson 1935

- Thoroughly mashed potatoes - 175g
- Melted butter - 60ml
- Caster sugar - 115g
- Currants - 90g
- Lemon peel - from 2 lemons grated fine
- Medium egg - 1
- Lemon essence - ¼ tsp
- Sweet shortcrust pastry (page 118)
- A little rum

- Stir all the ingredients together one way until thoroughly mixed.
- Line patty tins or small tins with pastry, then fill with the mixture and bake.
- When cooked, put a few drops of rum into each tartlet.

Me Ma's Mincemeat

I make this in September for the mince pies at Christmas. It improves with age.

- Butter - 225g shredded (freeze it before grating)
- Sultana (white) raisins - 150g
- Dark raisins - 150g
- Currants - 150g
- Green apples - 3 medium peeled, cored and chopped small
- English marmalade - 100ml
- Chopped almonds - 100g
- Brown sugar - 250ml
- Scotch whisky - 100ml
- Juice of ½ lemon
- Grated nutmeg - ¼ tsp
- Ground ginger - ½ tsp

- Mix everything together, cover with a cloth and leave it in a cool place overnight.
- Next day, pack into jars and seal.

Northumbrian Mince Pies

- Puff pastry - 500g (page 118)
- Me Ma's mincemeat - 450g (above)
- Egg white - 1 lightly beaten
- Caster sugar

- Roll the pastry out to about 5cm thick on a floured surface, and cut out 10cm circles You should get about 16-18.
- Place 1 tsp of mincemeat in the centre of each circle, brush the edges with egg white, then gather together tightly to completely encase the mincemeat.
- Turn the sealed edges underneath, then press them into round, flat pies.
- Using scissors, snip two small slits in the top of each pie, brush with egg white and sprinkle with caster sugar. Heat oven to 180°C and bake for 20 mins.

APPLES

Apples grow well in the Northern Counties, and there have been myriad recipes devised to use them up. Home made pies seem to come in two varieties; or maybe it would be more accurate to say that there are two distinct schools of apple pie making. Some families believe the crust is the thing, and the pie is mostly pastry with an apple flavour provided by the thin filling. Others believe the opposite, and the fruit occupies ninety per cent of their pie. Both can be excellent, but either way the major ingredient must be very, very good: the former must have wonderful pastry, and the latter wonderful fruit.

Prize-winning Apple Pie

The winning apple pie for several years at Wolsingham Fair, in Weardale—the oldest continuously running fair in the United Kingdom. I was initially refused this recipe by the woman who entered it as she feared I might be tempted to share it with her rivals, but afterwards she relented and told me the secret was that she added 'a few tablespoons of sour cream' to her pastry. It's a great pie, the Bramleys stay firm and sharp and the Granny Smiths bake soft and sweet. Let the pie cool completely before serving, and for the who prefer apple pie warm, just heat it up again.

- Bramley apples - 700g to 800g
- Granny Smith apples - 500g
- Fresh lemon juice- 2 tsp
- Light brown sugar - 120g packed
- White sugar - 50g plus 1 tbs
- Cornflour - 3 tbs
- Ground cinnamon - $\frac{1}{2}$ tsp
- Coarse salt - $\frac{1}{4}$ tsp
- Ground nutmeg - $\frac{1}{8}$ tsp
- Egg white - 1
- Unsalted butter - 2 tsp softened, plus 1 tbs. cold unsalted butter cut into small (1cm) cubes
- Plain flour - 25-40g
- Shortcrust Pastry (page 118)

Preheat the oven to 200°C.

- Filling: Peel the apples, slice in large pieces, place in a large bowl and toss with the lemon juice.
- Combine the brown sugar, 50g of the white sugar, cornflour, cinnamon, coarse salt, and nutmeg in a small bowl. Set aside.
- In a small dish, lightly beat egg white with 1 tsp water. Set aside.
- Butter a deep-sided pie plate with softened butter.
- Roll dough into a circle that's 5mm thick and about 55cm across.
- Lay the pastry in the pie plate, allowing about a 20cm overhang.
- Brush the bottom and sides of the dough with enough egg-white wash to coat.

- Pour the sugar and spice mix over apples, toss to coat. Mound the apples in the pie plate, and dot with bits of cold butter.
- Roll the remaining dough into a circle that's big enough to cover the pie and place over the filling. Flute the edge of the dough with lightly floured fingers.
- Brush the lid with cold water and sprinkle the surface with the remaining 1 tbs white sugar. Cut a steam vent in the lid and bake until the top and bottom crusts are golden brown and the juices are bubbling, 60 to 75 minutes.
- Cool the pie at least 3 hours before serving. You can reheat for a few minutes for those who like it hot.

Wilfra Tarts

Wilfra Tarts are a traditional apple and cheese bake made in Ripon, North Yorkshire in honour of St. Wilfrid, who built the cathedral in Ripon in the 7th Century. Each year, during the first week in August, the local townspeople used to make Wilfra Tarts and leave them on windowsills for passers-by to enjoy. I have seen them as open tarts, small cakes and individual pies. And yes, they are not authentic unless made with Wensleydale cheese.

- Sweet shortcrust pastry - 450g (page 118)

- Cooking apples - 3 peeled, cored and sliced
- Water - 2 tbs
- White sugar - 110g
- Wensleydale cheese - 110g sliced
- Caster sugar - 2 tsp

- Grease a 30cm x 20cm Swiss roll tin.
- Cook apples with water and sugar until soft. Strain and cool.
- Roll out half the pastry to make a rectangle and line the tin. Layer with apples and cheese.
- Roll out the remaining pastry and place on top to cover the pie. Seal the edges, leaving two steam holes in the centre.
- Bake in a preheated 90°C oven for 35 minutes until golden. Remove from the oven and sprinkle with caster sugar. Serve warm with cream or custard.

Sticky Toffee Pudding—Makes 12 individual puddings

Sticky toffee pudding was 'invented' in Cartmel, the picture book village south of the Lake District in Cumbria. You can find it on menus the world over since it shot to fame in the late 20th century.

- Pitted dried dates - 180g chopped
- Water - 240ml
- Butter - 60g
- Brown sugar - 160g firmly packed
- Vanilla extract - 8ml
- Medium eggs - 2
- Treacle - 40g
- Golden syrup - 30g
- Plain flour - 275g
- Baking powder - 8g
- Bicarbonate of soda - 2g

- Add the dates to the water in a small saucepan, bring to the boil and simmer over low heat for only 3 minutes. Remove from heat and let stand.
- Cream together the butter, brown sugar and vanilla.
- Add eggs, one at a time, beating well after each addition.
- Add the treacle and golden syrup and beat well.
- In another bowl, mix together the flour and baking powder.
- Add the dry ingredients to the creamed mixture a little at a time and beat until smooth after each addition.
- Puree the date mixture in a food processor or blender. Add in the baking soda, blend 30 seconds more then quickly pour this hot mixture into the other ingredients and mix until smooth.
- Pour into well greased and floured muffin tins and bake for about 18-20 minutes at 180°C until the centres are just firm.
- Serve warm with Toffee Sauce.

Toffee Sauce:
- Double cream - 125ml
- Butter - 60g
- Brown sugar - 60g firmly packed

- Treacle - 1 tbs
- Golden syrup - 2 tbs
- Vanilla extract - 2 tsp

- Bring all of the ingredients to a slow rolling boil for about 2 minutes before serving over the baked puddings.

Yorkshire Curd Pie

- Sweet shortcrust pastry (page 118)

- Fresh curds or cottage cheese - 175ml
- Heavy cream - 250ml
- Large eggs - 3
- Large egg yolks - 3
- White Sugar - 70g
- Rosewater - 2tbs
- Ground nutmeg - ½ tsp
- Ground cinnamon - ¼ tsp
- Currants - 40g

Preheat the oven to 230°C.
- Roll out pastry to a thickness of 3mm and fit it to a 25cm pie tin. Cut away the excess with a sharp knife or scissors, then prick the bottom of the pastry shell thoroughly.
- Fill the shell with baking weights and blind bake for 7-10 minutes then remove the weights and continue baking for another 8-10 minutes or until the crust is lightly browned.

Lower the oven temp to 180°C.

filling:
- In a small saucepan, gently heat the cream.
- In a mixing bowl, beat together the eggs, egg yolks, sugar, rosewater, and the spices until frothy—about 5 minutes.
- Over a large mixing bowl, press the cottage cheese through a sieve, beat until smooth then add the egg mixture and blend

well. Add the hot cream slowly to the cheese mixture and beat until well blended.

- Stir in the currants and pour mixture into the prepared crust.
- Bake for about 30 minutes, then allow to cool. Chill and sprinkle with cinnamon.

Startforth Gingerbread

Startforth is a part of Barnard Castle on the banks of the River Tees. Other than the name, the origins of this recipe are lost to time.

- Butter - 115g
- Brown sugar - 60g
- Treacle - 225g
- Plain flour - 225g
- Bicarbonate of soda - ½ tsp
- Mixed spice - 1 tsp
- Pinch ground ginger - pinch
- Eggs - 2 beaten
- Sour milk - 60ml

- Set oven to 180°C
- Grease and line a 450g loaf tin.
- Melt the butter, sugar and treacle in a pan over low heat.
- Sift together the flour and bicarbonate of soda, mixed spice and ginger and stir the flour mixture into the treacle mixture.
- Add the beaten eggs and sour milk and mix thoroughly. Pour into the tin and bake for 1½ to 2 hours or until a skewer inserted comes out clean.
- Turn out on to a wire rack and cut into slices when cold.

BULLETS AND BISCUITS

Bullets is a Northern Counties name for candy or sweets, although it varies across the region—sometimes 'kets' sometimes 'spice' sometimes just 'sweeties' but among children and adults alike, they're always welcome. Whenever company turns up, or even if we just stop for a break and a cup of tea, there will almost always be a biscuit or two to accompany it. Dunking is optional.

Chocolate Spuds—make about 36

This is the original recipe from Hartlepool. I find it better to use hot chocolate mix instead of cocoa powder. The cinnamon is optional, but it's good!

- Warm mashed potatoes - 200g
- Butter - 1 tbs
- Salt - a pinch
- Vanilla extract - 1 tsp
- Icing sugar - 450g sifted
- Shredded coconut - 350g
- Cocoa powder - 30g
- Cinnamon - ½ tsp

- Line a baking sheet with foil or waxed paper.
- In a large bowl beat together the potatoes, butter, salt, and vanilla extract.
- Beat in the icing sugar a little at a time, then add the coconut and mix thoroughly.
- Take teaspoons of the mixture and form into potato shapes, place each on the baking sheet. Chill until set, about 1 hour.
- Mix together the cocoa and cinnamon, roll the spuds in the coating and they are ready to eat.

Great Aunty Ada's Taffee *(from Ros Kellock)*

"This recipe was given to me as a child in the late 1960s by maternal great Aunty Ada from Penshaw, who was then aged in her 90s."

- Sugar - 450g
- Butter - 115g
- Water - 125ml
- Malt vinegar - 1 tbs

- Melt all ingredients in a pan, boil for 20 minutes or until set.
- Test set by dropping into a saucer of cold water, if it hardens then it's ready.

Cinder Toffee

"…This recipe is taken from memory as it is nearly 50 years since I saw my mother make cinder toffee." - Peggy Hutchinson circa 1935 (This recipe is verbatim with the addition of my metric measures)

- Sugar - 350g
- Water - 250ml
- Bicarbonate of soda - 1 tsp

- Boil the sugar and cold water for about 20 minutes. Have a deep bowl of cold water standing ready.
- Add the bicarbonate of soda to the boiling toffee as you lift it from the fire. The toffee then boils up rather like milk boiling over and you pour it into the bowl of cold water.
- When cold, take it out of the water and place in a tin or dish. It makes quite a lot of toffee and is crunchy.

Dainty Dinahs—makes about 60

Horner's sweets were made at Chester-le-Street in County Durham from 1914 until 1960. The history of candy making on the site goes back way farther than that though, and the most famous of the confections they made was this soft caramel. I remember these from my childhood as my grandmother would use them as enticement for completing chores. The following is an easy recipe that makes excellent caramels that never last long.

- Butter - 450g
- Golden syrup - 325g
- Sweetened condensed milk - 325g
- Light brown sugar - 900g
- Vanilla essence - 1 tbs

- Place all ingredients in a heavy saucepan with tall sides.
- Cook on medium-low heat until the butter and sugar melt, making sure to scrape down the sides.

- On medium heat, gradually bring up to 118°C on a candy thermometer, stirring often.
- Quickly remove from heat and add vanilla.
- Pour into well buttered baking sheet.
- When set but still lukewarm, turn onto a cutting board and cut into oblongs and wrap in wax paper.

Kendal Mint Cake

Probably the most famous regional candy, famously taken to the top of Everest by Edmund Hillary, Kendall Mint Cake is considered a very high energy food, although nutritionally it is somewhat wanting as it consists mostly of sugar. It has become a de rigour food with the outdoors enthusiasts, as it weighs very little and does not take up much space. It is easy to make with just three ingredients.

- White sugar - 450g
- Milk - 150ml
- Peppermint essence - 1 tsp

- Place the milk and sugar into a large saucepan over low heat and stir until sugar dissolves.
- Bring mixture to the boil until temperature reaches 114°C on candy thermometer.
- Remove from the heat and beat vigorously for 2 minutes.
- Return to the heat and raise temperature to 119°C - remove from heat immediately.
- Add peppermint essence, stirring quickly, then pour into a well-greased shallow tin.
- Mark into squares and when set, break into individual pieces.

Newton Butterscotch

I tried hard to discover which Newton this butterscotch is named after as we have a plethora of places so named in the Northern Counties—Newton Aycliffe and Archdeacon Newton in County Durham, Newton-in-Furness in Cumbria, Newton-le-Willows and Newton-under-Roseberry in North Yorkshire, and in Northumberland, Newton-by-the-sea and plain old Newton. You choose.

- Sugar - 350g
- Water - 250ml
- Black treacle -150g
- Vegetable oil - 1 tbs
- Butter - 100g
- Brown sugar - 1 tbs

- Place all the ingredients in a large pan. Bring to boil over low heat until it snaps in cold water.
- Pour into a buttered tin and mark squares before it sets. Break into pieces once cold.

Coconut Ice

This is the home made sweet that appeared with regularity at garden fetes, Women's Institute stalls and church hall sales all over the Northern Counties, and I daresay the entire country. It still makes an occasional appearance but it has fallen from favour because it is very old fashioned.

- Sweetened condensed milk - 250g
- Icing sugar - 250g
- Desiccated coconut - 200g
- Red food colouring, optional

- Using a wooden spoon, mix together the condensed milk and icing sugar in a large bowl until very stiff. Work the coconut into the mix until well combined.
- Divide the mix into two and knead a very small amount of colouring into one half to make it pink. Dust a board with icing sugar, then shape each half into equal sized rectangles and

place one on top of the other. Roll out until you have a rectangle of two-colour coconut ice about 3cm thick.

- Leave on a flat surface uncovered for at least 3 hours or ideally overnight to set. Cut into squares with a sharp knife and pack into bags or boxes. Will keep for a month when stored in an airtight container.

BISCUITS

Grasmere Gingerbread

Another famous recipe from Cumbria, this time from Grasmere. This is a cross between biscuit and cake. The claim is that it was invented by Sarah Nelson way back in 1854, but a little digging reveals that Sarah refined recipes she had herself collected from other parts of the county to come up with this definitive version. Incidentally, when Sarah lived there, Grasmere was in Lancashire but is now in Cumbria since the county boundaries were redrawn in 1974.

- Plain flour - 110g
- Fine oatmeal - 110g
- Brown sugar - 110g
- Ground ginger - 1 tsp
- Baking powder - $\frac{1}{4}$ tsp
- Butter - 150g well-chilled

- Mix all the dry ingredients together well in a bowl.
- Grate the chilled butter into the bowl, a little at a time, stirring to keep the pieces separate. Rub the butter and dry ingredients together until you get a bread crumb consistency.
- Shake this mixture evenly into a lightly greased and floured 25cm x 20cm baking pan and tamp it down lightly.
- Bake in the centre of a 180°C oven for about 45 minutes or until the mixture is just firm in the centre when lightly pressed.
- Cool for 5 minutes then turn it out onto a wire rack and leave it to get quite cold.
- Cut the gingerbread into oblongs wedges. Store in an airtight container.

Stanhope Firelighters

The original recipe for Stanhope Firelighters is just oatmeal, sugar and margarine. I have updated this one to be more like the 'power bars' that fell walkers and others who enjoy the outdoors take along because they are a light-weight source of quick energy. They were so named because they are the same shape as the paraffin soaked firelighters used to light coal fires in the old days.

• Soft brown sugar - 100g
• Butter - 100g
• Golden syrup - 1 tbs
• Rolled oats - 200g
• Desiccated coconut - 25g
• Baking powder - 1 tsp
• Sultana raisins - 75g
• Salt - pinch

- Melt the butter, sugar and golden syrup in a saucepan, then stir in the remaining ingredients.
- Press into a 28cm x18cm shallow baking tin.
- Bake for 20 minutes in a preheated 180°C oven.
- Remove from oven and immediately cut into oblongs and leave to cool.

Whittingham Buttons

So named because they look like coat buttons. The original recipe came from Northumberland in the 20th century, so a fairly recent innovation as we can see from the use of custard powder, although that was invented in Birmingham by chemist Sir Alfred Bird in 1837 for his wife who was allergic to eggs. Creamy and light they go well with a cup of tea, although they don't dunk well!

• Butter - 175g
• Icing sugar - 75g
• Plain flour - 175g
• Custard powder - 50g

- Cream butter and icing sugar until light and fluffy.
- Mix in flour and custard powder to form a firm dough.

- Roll spoonfuls of this mixture into a balls the size of a walnut.
- Place onto a lightly greased baking tray and flatten slightly.
- Bake at 180°C for 10-15 mins until golden. Poke four holes with a toothpick in each to resemble buttonholes.
- Cool on a wire rack.

North Riding Gingersnaps

These gingersnaps make a perfect base for Gurney Valley cheesecake (page 126) and Peach Eggs (page 124)

- Plain flour - 225g
- Sugar - 115g
- Butter - 115g
- Golden syrup - 115g
- Bicarbonate of soda - 1 tsp
- Ground ginger - 1½ tsp
- Fresh ginger - 1 tbs grated

- Melt butter over a low heat and add the sugar and golden syrup then all other ingredients.
- Shape into small balls and flatten slightly with a fork, then place onto a greased baking tray.
- Bake 15 minutes in a 160°C oven.

Oatmeal Biscuits—About 30 small, 15 large or 8 huge biscuits

The finer the oatmeal, the finer the biscuit. Perfect for Peach Eggs (page 124)

- Oatmeal - 500g
- Baking powder - 5 tsp
- Plain flour - 400g
- Butter - 370g
- White sugar - 150g
- Milk - 500ml

- Melt butter, add sugar and milk. Pour this over the oatmeal and let it stand for an hour.

- Mix baking powder in a little of the flour and mix this into the oatmeal mixture. Knead enough flour into the mass so the dough can can be rolled out to about 4mm.
- Cut out round biscuits with a glass or cut dough into squares. Prick the biscuits with fork.
- Bake the biscuits in the oven at 185°C for about 12-15 minutes.
- Cool on wire rack. Store in tight box or tin.

Jimmy-jams—about 50

These turn up all over the English speaking world with variations on the name ... Jim-jams, Jimmy-jams, Jam-jams ... but before they got the hole and became Jammy Dodgers here in the Northern Counties they were called Jimmy-jams. My favourite jam for these is actually plum jelly, but use any jam for the filling and they will still be as good.

- Butter - 340g
- Brown sugar - 200g
- Golden syrup - 170g
- Eggs - 2
- Rind of a lemon - finely grated
- Plain flour - 380g
- Baking powder - 2 tsp

- Cream together butter, sugar and syrup, add eggs and grated lemon rind and mix well.
- In another bowl mix dry ingredients. Stir into wet ingredients until combined.
- Roll out dough fairly thin, about 3mm and cut out rounds with a 45mm cutter.
- Place on pans, you can place them quite close together, they don't spread very much.
- Bake in 190°C oven for 6 minutes.
- Cool completely.
- When cool put a teaspoonful of jam on one biscuit and sandwich with another one.

Windermere Crackers

These are plain but delicious. You can fancy them up by adding sesame seeds to the mix, a teaspoonful of nutritional yeast, or a smidgeon of garlic powder, or a little grated parmesan cheese.

- Plain flour - 350g
- Salt - 1 tsp
- Vegetable oil - 60ml
- Water - 200ml

- Cut a piece of baking parchment paper to fit a shallow baking tray then set aside.
- In a large bowl combine the flour and salt.
- Stir the oil into the water, the stir this into the flour and bring together to form a dough.
- Roll out the dough on a well floured surface until it is about 1-2mm thick and the same size as the parchment paper.
- Place the dough on the parchment paper, prick all over with a fork to stop it rising too much and mark into squares or rectangles.
- Carefully slide the parchment paper onto the baking tray and place it in the preheated 220°C oven.
- Cook until crisp and golden (10-15 min). Keep an eye on them as they may need longer.
- Transfer the crackers to a wire rack until cool enough to handle.
- Leave to cool completely then break into individual crackers.
- They will keep fresh up to 2 weeks in an airtight container.

PICKLES, PRESERVES AND CONDIMENTS

What a rare day it would be to go into my refrigerator and find no pickles. My last inventory included onions, asparagus, beets, wild mushrooms, and pears— all prettily pickled and beckoning. In addition, there was ketchup—both mushroom and tomato—two types of chutney and even a little dish of scallops and shrimps pickling away in an overnight bath of fresh lime juice. How the first Roman soldiers that patrolled Hadrian's Wall must have looked forward to

a bowl of steamy soup at the end of a long January shift! And how glad they must have been for the pepper they'd introduced to Britain to ensure the soup hit the spot. Mint sauce and rosemary might well have come in with the Romans, although they may have already been there. Included too are some strange condiments that you're unlikely to see on a restaurant menu but are still made in Northumberland homes every Autumn when the right ingredients come into season.

The Northern Counties has generated a surprising number of condiments, especially from the heavy industrial areas of mining and shipbuilding. Sunderland Spice—once a ubiquitous item of many pantries—is used to add depth of flavour to many creations and features prominently in pickles, preserved meats and fish. Durham was once synonymous with mustard and what baked ham would be complete without Cumberland Sauce?

MUSTARD

"About 1720 a Mrs. Clements of Durham, England, originated a process of making a fine powder of mustard seed. The Ainsley Company of Durham (founded 1717), which used this process, made the name of Durham synonymous with mustard. When Colman's of Norwich (originated about 1814) adopted a trademark for its Durham Mustard in 1855, it chose the head of the shorthorn, or Durham, bull." ~ A History of Durham, North Carolina: Jean Bradley Anderson 1990

Aficionados of mustard the world over are familiar with the story of Mrs. Clements of Durham who figured out a new method of grinding mustard seeds to a fine powder. Previously, mustard was simply ground in a mortar and pestle with a little vinegar or wine to make a paste. I believe Mrs. Clements dry-ground desiccated seeds then winnowed the coarse chaff then reground through successively finer millstones and finally bolted it through cloth resulting in the powder we know today. What I find hard to believe it that no one thought of it before that, and I'll go out on limb and guess that the famous 'Durham Mustard' was in fact the powder plus other spices and salt that facilitated the making of a superior paste with just the addition of water and none of the tedious grinding.

"A Considerable quantity of mustard is sown in the neighbourhood of York, and fields of it may be met with in other parts of the Riding. It is prepared for use in the city of York, where there are mills and machinery for the purpose; and it is afterwards sold under the name of Durham Mustard; being prepared after the manner there practised, or as was there first done."

[Agricultural Surveys: Yorkshire, North-Riding, 1800]

Adulteration of Mustard. "Genuine mustard, either in powder, or in the state of a paste ready for use, is perhaps rarely to be met with in the shops. The article sold under the name of genuine Durham Mustard, is usually a mixture of mustard and common wheaten flour, with a portion of Cayenne pepper, and a large quantity of bay salt, made with water into a paste, ready for use. Some manufacturers adulterate their mustard with radish seed and pease flour. The salt and Cayenne pepper contribute materially to the keeping of ready-made mustard, sold in pots."

[A Treatise on Adulterations of Food. London: 1820]

Whatever she did, she became the culinary star of her day following praise for her product from no less a person than the pudding king himself, King George I. I visited the shop that is said to have been Mrs Clement's in Saddler Street in Durham City and bought a modern mustard, which, while nice enough, was not as good as this one I devised based on my take of the original.

Mustard is a member of the brassica family, like cabbages, turnips and radishes. The heat from mustard comes from an enzyme—myrosin—that reacts when wetted. And the wetting agent is of principal importance when making mustard as different mediums cause different degrees of heat. Milk gives the mildest heat, then wine, beer and water in that order. This recipe for mustard is well worth making—essential in fact to making many authentic recipes in this book—and constitutes the third form of Europe's great triumvirate: Dijon, Dusseldorf and Durham.

Durham Mustard

Durham Mustard used to be the name given to all dry ground mustard powder throughout the 18th and 19th centuries. This version is a 'made' mustard, the recipe for which is based on extensive research I have done into 'Mrs Clements of Durham' over thirty years. The celebrated Mrs Clements is acknowledged as the person who figured out how to make dry mustard powder, whereas previously mustard had been a wet paste ground directly from seeds, or coarse ground like many continental mustards are still. As a member of a miller's family, she probably winnowed the coarse chaff then bolted the remaining fine powder.

- Dry cider - 500ml
- Onion - 2 chopped
- Honey - 3 tbs
- Coarse salt - 1 tsp
- Garlic clove 1 crushed
- Juniper berries - 4 crushed
- Mustard powder - 220g
- Vegetable oil - 1 tbs

- Combine the cider, onion, juniper and garlic in a small saucepan, bring to the boil for 5 minutes then remove from heat and allow to cool completely.
- Strain out solids, add mustard and oil and whisk until smooth.
- Return to the heat and as soon as the mixture comes to a boil, remove pan from heat. Leave uncovered for 1 minute, then cover pan with a lid and set aside until cool.
- Chill and put into a small airtight jar. Allow to mature for 2 weeks before use.

Elder Mustard

I'm fairly certain this mustard recipe survived in part due to its astonishing colour. The Northallerton woman who passed this on to me said her mother, who died 'the same day as Pope John' (June 3, 1963) made it for years and served it on cheese sandwiches.

- Yellow mustard seeds - 250g
- Black mustard seeds - 250g

- White vinegar - 1 litre
- Coarse salt - 30g
- Fresh elderberries - 100g mashed and pushed through a sieve to remove seeds.

- Grind half the mustard seeds to a powder and place in a non-metallic pot with the whole seeds and the vinegar.
- Soak for 24 hours in the vinegar. Then add the salt and the elderberries.
- Place in sterile jars with non-corrosive lids and keep one week before use. Store in a cool place.

Marsden Mustard

A coarse grained mustard that has been formulated especially to go with grilled sausages, and in particular those served on Batten Buns (page 177).

- Brown mustard seeds - 250g
- Yellow mustard seeds - 60g
- Dark beer (stout, porter, etc.) - 240ml
- White wine vinegar - 300ml
- Mustard powder - 250g combined with 240ml water and allowed to stand for 20 minutes
- Sugar - 1 tsp
- Salt - 1 tsp
- Ground allspice - 1 tsp
- Ground turmeric - $\frac{1}{4}$ tsp
- Ground mace - $\frac{1}{4}$ tsp

- In a non-reactive container, combine mustard seeds with beer and vinegar. Let sit for 48 hours.
- Check periodically to make sure that seeds are still covered by liquid. Add more vinegar if necessary.
- Transfer seeds and liquid to a food processor. Add remaining ingredients. Process until seeds become creamy.

Bishopton Chutney

This makes what might be described as basic chutney familiar to many who enjoy the brown fruity condiment that was popular following the Second World War when dried fruit and sugar become more readily available. This recipe comes courtesy of the Women's Institute.

- Apples - 1kg peeled, cored and chopped
- Raisins - 450g chopped
- Garlic - 100g sliced thin
- Sugar - 450g
- Malt vinegar - 450ml
- Salt - 1 tsp
- Ground ginger - ½ tsp
- White pepper - pinch

- Place the apples, garlic, sugar, raisins and vinegar in a large saucepan and bring to a simmer. Cook until brown and thick.
- Add the salt, ginger and pepper and stir well.
- Pack into clean, jars and seal as you would for jam.

Haswell Pickle

Very simple, lovely crunchy pickle excellent on a cheese sandwich.

- Swede turnip - 1 medium, diced small
- Sweet onion - 1 medium, diced small
- Enough Brown Sauce (page 159) to cover generously

- Put everything into a pot and bring to the boil. Simmer 5 minutes.
- Pack into sterile jars and seal.

Keeps indefinitely. Refrigerate once opened.

Ted's Goosegob Chutney

My brother loved the sour tang of gooseberries so much he would pick and eat the ones my dad grew long before they were ripe. If you are fortunate enough to grow your own gooseberries, this is a wonderful condiment to accompany cheese. Or buy seasonal gooseberries when they come available in the shops.

- Seedless raisins - 350g
- Medium onions - 3 peeled and chopped small
- Gooseberries - 900g topped and tailed
- Cider vinegar - 500ml
- Salt - pinch
- Brown sugar - 225g
- Cayenne pepper - $\frac{1}{2}$ tsp
- Ground ginger - 2 tbs

- Chop raisins and onions, place all ingredients into a saucepan and bring to the boil. Turn down the heat and simmer until tender and thick, about an hour.
- Place in jars and process.

Stanhope Mustard Pickle

The Weardale version of piccalilli.

- Cauliflower - 1 chopped fine
- Medium onions - 2 chopped fine
- Salt - 1 tsp
- Plain flour - 2 tbs
- Sugar - 60g
- Mustard powder - 1 tsp
- Turmeric - $\frac{1}{2}$ tsp
- Malt vinegar - 200ml

- Salt the vegetables and set aside for two days.
- Mix the flour, sugar, mustard and turmeric to a paste with a little cold vinegar.

- Boil the rest of the vinegar in a saucepan and pour it onto the paste, the return it all to the saucepan and stir over heat until it thickens.
- Shake off the surplus salt from the vegetables and add them to the pan. Simmer gently for 5 minutes then pour into jars, process and seal. Keep two weeks before using.

Wolviston Pickle

Yet another fine old recipe from Peggy Hutchinson's collection.

- Onions - 1kg
- Vegetable marrow - 1kg
- Cauliflower sprigs - 1kg
- Salt
- Malt vinegar - about 1 litre
- Pickling spice - 1 tbs (page 164)
- Turmeric - pinch
- Mustard powder 100g
- Plain flour - 15g

- Dice onions and marrow. Salt the vegetables and set them aside for two days. Shake off surplus salt, place in saucepan with spices in a muslin bag and cover with vinegar.
- Simmer until vegetables are soft. Remove spice bag and add turmeric.
- Mix mustard and flour to a thin paste with cold vinegar and add to the pan. Stir well and bring to boil.
- Simmer gently for 5 minutes then pour into jars, process and seal. Keep two weeks before using.

Pickled Red Cabbage

The classic accompaniment for many traditional dishes.

- Firm red cabbage - 1 small, quartered and shredded
- Salt - for layering
- Malt vinegar - 600ml

- Mace - $\frac{1}{2}$ tsp
- Allspice - 1 tbs, whole
- Cloves - 3 whole
- Ground cinnamon - $\frac{1}{4}$ tsp
- Black peppercorns - 15
- Bay leaves - 3

- Layer the shredded cabbage with salt. Leave overnight. Rinse and drain thoroughly.
- Bring the remaining ingredients to the boil, remove from the heat. Allow to cool and infuse for at least 2 hours before straining.
- Pack the cabbage into jars, cover with the vinegar and seal with non-corrosive lids.

This will keep for a month, after which the cabbage will lose its crispness and colour.

Pickled Beetroot

A marvellous pickled vegetable with superb red colouring.

- Malt vinegar - 1.1 litres
- Bay leaf - 2g
- Cinnamon stick - 1
- Allspice berries - 12
- Black peppercorns - 8g
- Mustard seeds - 8g
- Cloves - 4 whole
- Chilli pepper – 1
- Root ginger - 15g sliced
- Beetroots - small, evenly sized or larger beetroot sliced
- Salt

- Put the vinegar and all the spices in a large non-reactive saucepan (not an unlined copper or brass or iron one) and heat gently, covered tightly, until the point of simmering.
- Remove from the heat. Leave for 3 hours, and then strain through muslin or a jelly bag.

- Cook the unpeeled beetroots in boiling heavily salted water (1 tbs to 1 litre) until tender.
- Drain and allow them to cool. Skin them. Pack, without bruising, into jars. Cover well with cold pickling vinegar. Add 1 teaspoon salt to each 1kg jar.
- Seal and store.

Pickled Blackberries—Makes 4 x 450g jars

Blackberries are the great free food of the hedgerows, abundant and available for a long season. The tradition is you can pick blackberries until Michaelmas (Sept 29th) but on that day the devils spits on them. Or worse.

- Blackberries - 1 kg
- White wine vinegar - 300ml
- Sugar - 450g

- Wash and pick over the blackberries. Put the vinegar into a stainless steel pan with the sugar and heat gently, stirring until it dissolves. Add the blackberries and simmer gently for 5 minutes. Do not allow the fruit to become too soft or to break up.
- Remove the blackberries with a slotted spoon and pack into hot, dry, sterile jars with non-metal lids. Keep warm. Boil the vinegar and sugar until it is syrupy and pour the hot syrup over the fruit to cover completely. Seal. Store at least a week before eating.

Pickled Eggs

These are often found in pubs and are a great snack to go with beer. Refrigerated they will keep for weeks.

- White wine vinegar - 600ml, or cider vinegar or malt vinegar
- Pickling spice - 25g (page 164)
- Eggs - 6, hard boiled and shelled

- Put all the ingredients except the eggs in a heavy-based saucepan. Bring to the boil, then reduce the heat, cover and simmer gently for 10 minutes. Leave to cool, then strain some of the spiced vinegar into a large wide-mouthed jar.

- Put in the eggs and top up the jar with more spiced vinegar.
- Cover with airtight vinegar-proof tops and leave for 4-6 weeks to mature.

Variation: I have made beautiful gift jars using tiny quail eggs, which I got from a gamekeeper—perhaps you know one—or you can often buy them from Asian markets. Pickle these in raspberry vinegar without the spices.

SAUCES

Brown Sauce

A simple to make recipe using ordinary fruit from the garden. A slightly sweeter brown sauce than the commercial varieties.

- Purple plums - 6 chopped but not peeled
- Apples - 3 medium cored and chopped but not peeled
- Onions - 2 large peeled and chopped

- Place everything in a saucepan, add a little water, boil until soft then purée (easy if you use a blender). Then add:

- Malt vinegar - 1 litre
- Ground ginger, nutmeg, allspice, cayenne pepper - ½ tsp each
- Coarse salt - 50g
- White sugar - 600g

- Mix and simmer for about 2 hours. Put into jars and process to seal.

Red Sauce (Ketchup)

Ketchup is universally accepted as being made from tomatoes, but long before tomatoes were the most familiar base, ketchup was a thin, highly-flavoured condiment based on mushrooms and more like modern Worcestershire sauce than the thick, red, viscous sauce beloved of children the world over. I have simplified the process and ingredients for this delicious and easy-to-make version.

- Tomato paste - 160ml
- Golden syrup - 125ml
- White vinegar - 125ml
- Water - 60ml
- Sugar - 1 tbs
- Salt - 1 tsp
- Onion powder - ¼ tsp
- Garlic powder - ⅛ tsp

- Combine all ingredients in a medium saucepan over medium heat. Whisk until smooth.
- When mixture comes to a boil, reduce heat and simmer for 20 minutes, stirring often.
- Remove pan from heat and cover until cool. Chill and store in a covered container.

Bread Sauce

One of Dorothy Slightholme's best-loved traditional sauces from Yorkshire. Serve with roast poultry or game.

- Onion - 1 peeled
- Cloves - 2
- Bay leaf - 1
- Milk - 450ml
- Fresh white breadcrumbs - 75g
- Butter - 15g
- Single cream - 2 tbs

- Stick 2 cloves into the onion and put in a saucepan with the bay leaf and milk.
- Bring slowly to the boil, remove from the heat, cover and leave to infuse for 10 minutes, then remove the bay leaf and onion.
- Add the breadcrumbs, return to the heat, cover and simmer for 10-15 minutes, stirring occasionally.
- Stir in the butter and cream and serve immediately.

Cumberland Sauce

There is debate as to whether this sauce was named for the old county or the Duke that won the Battle of Culloden. Either way, it has become the classic accompaniment to baked ham, but it also goes perfectly with venison or lamb.

- Orange - 1 zest and juice
- Lemon - 1 zest and juice
- Redcurrant jelly - 4 tbs
- Durham Mustard - 1 tsp (page 152)
- Port - 4 tbs
- Ground ginger – ½ tsp

- Cover the orange and lemon zest with water, simmer for 5 minutes and drain.
- Place the orange and lemon juices, zest, redcurrant jelly and mustard in a pan and heat gently, stirring continuously, until the jelly has melted. Simmer for 5 minutes then remove from the heat and add the port and ginger. Serve hot.

Curry Sauce

The first time I had curry sauce on my chips instead of vinegar was in Darlington. I was dubious at first, and then won over. Since those days it has become a commonplace offering all over the country. You can, of course, make your own curry powder.

- Onion - 1 chopped
- Apple - 1 chopped
- Curry powder - 1 tbs
- Vegetable oil - 2 tbs
- Plain flour - 2 tbs
- Water - 600ml
- Tomato purée - 1 tbs
- Salt, pepper and lemon juice

- Fry the onion and apple with the curry powder in the vegetable oil until tender.

- Stir in the flour, cook for 2 minutes and then remove from the heat and add the water, tomato purée, salt, pepper and lemon juice to taste. Simmer for 15 minutes.

Choppy Sauce

Mint grows well in the North of England and almost every garden has it. This is a common sauce for lamb all over the Northern Counties and this version comes from High Etherley in County Durham.

- English mint - 1 bunch
- Onion - 1 small or 2 scallions, chopped fine
- Salt - pinch
- Boiling water - 4 tbs
- Malt vinegar - 4 tbs
- White sugar - 1 tsp

- Wash the mint leaves, sprinkle with salt and chop finely.
- Place into a small bowl, add the sugar and pour in the boiling water, stir and leave to cool.
- Add the vinegar. Adjust salt, sugar, water or vinegar to taste.

Haswell Hot Sauce

This old-fashioned sauce has a depth of flavour less fiery than modern chilli pepper hot sauces. It's named for a Haswell Plough friend who loves hot sauce, but it doesn't love him back.

- Malt vinegar - 500ml
- Treacle - 2 tbs
- Plain flour - 2 tbs
- Mustard powder - 1 tbs
- Sugar - 3 tbs
- Salt - 1 tsp
- Pickling spice - 30g (page 164)

- Mix all together, boil for 20 minutes. Strain and bottle when cold.

VINEGAR

> *"A loaf of bread," the Walrus said,*
> *"Is what we chiefly need:*
> *Pepper and vinegar besides*
> *Are very good indeed -*
> *Now, if you're ready, Oysters dear,*
> *We can begin to feed."*

Flavoured vinegar has been an important ingredient in Northern Counties cooking since medieval times both for flavour and for preserving food. Nearly all farmhouse kitchens had a vinegar barrel, kept well away from the fermenting beer and country wines. In the Autumn, when new wine was made and last year's wines were ready for consumption, a quantity of wine would be set aside for vinegar. Many chose to use up stale beer in this manner but those requiring a stronger product for preserving purposes opted for wine vinegar made from the bounty of the hedgerow.

Some of the vinegar was used as soon as it was ready, but some was kept until the garden herbs were at their most pungent, just before flowering. Tarragon, basil, thyme and fruit—particularly raspberries—were used to flavour the vinegar.

Basic Flavoured Vinegar

The simplest of all condiments.

- White wine vinegar - 1 litre
- Shallots - 4 peeled and sliced
- Yellow mustard seed - 2 tbs
- Tarragon, basil, thyme, etc. - 1 large bunch, or
- Raspberries - 1 litre

- Bruise the flavouring ingredient and steep for three weeks in the vinegar.
- If you're in a hurry, you may heat the vinegar gently and steep the ingredients for an hour or so. The longer, cold method produces superior vinegar.
- Remove the flavouring ingredient and discard.

- Bottle in sound bottles that have been thoroughly cleaned and sterilized.

Important: If you intend to use the vinegar for preserves (pickled onions, chutney, etc.) you must use vinegar of at least 7% acetic acid.

Sunderland Spice Mix

"Excellent for flavouring meat, stews, pies, game, potted meat and fish paste" - Peggy Hutchinson

- Ground black pepper - 25g
- Ground nutmeg - 12g
- Ground cloves - 12g
- Ground mace - 12g
- Ground Cayenne pepper - 6g

- Mix all the ingredients together and store in an airtight container.

Pickling Spice

- Black peppercorns - 2 tbs
- Yellow mustard seed - 2 tbs
- Coriander seeds - 2 tbs
- Allspice berries - 1 tbs
- Bay leaves - 2 crumbled
- Red pepper flakes - 1 tbs crushed

- Place all ingredients in a small glass jar, shake to combine.

Yorkshire Relish

From the 1930's collection of the Yorkshire Observer (Mrs. Scargill, Batley).

- Cloves - 15g
- Cayenne pods - 7g
- Black peppercorns - 30g
- Water - 240ml

- Boil 20 minutes, then add:

- Vinegar - 1 litre
- White sugar - 225g
- Salt - 12g
- Gravy browning - 2 tbs

- Boil altogether for 5 min. Strain and it is ready for use when cold.

Durham Salad Cream (page 4)

JAM AND JELLY

Gooseberry Jam— Makes 4 x 250ml jars

Gooseberries, like leeks today, once commanded the attention of maniacal growers in the Northern Counties. In the North Yorkshire village of Egton Bridge there is still a gooseberry show, which has been held annually for more than 200 years. A local restaurant once spotlighted gooseberries during the show with a special menu including gooseberry and stilton wrapped in filo pastry, for starter, pan-fried sole fillets accompanied by gooseberry veronique sauce for main course and baked gooseberry and almond tart served with crème Anglaise for dessert.

The world record was set by Tom Ventress in 1952 with a berry weighing 30 drams & 8 grains—55g or nearly 2 ounces—the size of a chicken egg.

- Gooseberries - 1.5kg
- Water - 600ml
- White sugar - 1.8kg

- Top and tail the gooseberries.
- In a preserving pan, combine the gooseberries and water and cook over a low heat for 2 hours until the contents of the pan have reduced by a third. Mash the fruit.
- Preheat the oven to 190°C. Pour the sugar into a baking tray.
- Bake the sugar in the oven until hot to the touch. Do not allow the sugar to caramelize. Remove from the oven.

- Add the warmed sugar to the fruit, increase the heat and stir until the sugar has dissolved. Bring the jam to the boil and begin testing for the setting point by placing a drop of jam onto a cold plate. If the jam wrinkles when you push it with your finger, it is ready.
- Skim the jam if necessary and transfer into sterilized jam jars. Seal immediately and leave undisturbed overnight in a cool, dark place to set.

Redcar Apricot Jam

This is more accurately a jelly because it is strained through a jelly bag. You may save the first step by using apple juice, but if you go that route you will need to use pectin to thicken the jelly. This recipe is a little vague on boil time but that's because the quantities of juice will also be uncertain.

- Dried apricots - 500g
- Apples - 1.5kg
- Water - enough to cover the apricots
- Sugar - measure for measure with the juice

- Cut up the apricots, cover them with water and let steep 48 hours.
- Cut up the apples (don't peel or core, this is where the pectin is, which allows the jelly to set), cover with water and boil to a pulp. Allow to cool, then strain and squeeze out all the juice.
- Run the apple juice through a jelly bag, without squeezing, to clear it.
- Add the apple juice, apricots and water together.
- Measure the juice and to every cupful of pulp add one cupful of sugar and boil in the usual way until set. Testing for the setting point by placing a drop of jam onto a cold plate. If the jam wrinkles when you push it with your finger, it is ready.

Blackberry Jam

This jam is made without added pectin and relies on that already in the fruit. The earlier in the season you pick them, the more pectin they'll have. I think everyone has memories from childhood of picking blackberries in the late Summer. Most of ours went into pies, some into wine, but quite a lot went into jam too. This recipes is somewhere between a jam and a jelly and is softer than that you'd get from a shop.

- Blackberries - 1kg
- White sugar (see note) - 400g
- Fresh lemon juice - 2 tbs

- Put the blackberries, sugar and lemon juice into a large saucepan, making sure there is sufficient headspace to allow for foaming.
- Heat over medium-low and simmer the jam until it reaches gel stage, stirring to keep the bubbles down. In this lower sugar recipe it should take 20-30 minutes (note—increasing the sugar will make a jam that gels faster but is very sweet).
- Test for gel stage on a plate in the freezer. A spoonful dropped onto the cold plate should wrinkle when pushed with a finger.
- When ready, pour jam into prepared jars, leaving 1cm headspace. Store in the refrigerator, or process in a water bath canner for 5 minutes and store in the cupboard.

Cumberland Rum Butter

An odd old-fashioned conserve that was traditionally spread on toast or buttered bread at Christmastime and at Christenings throughout Cumberland. In farming communities it was called 'brown jam.' It was often made with brandy instead of rum.

- Butter 175g
- Brown sugar - 175g
- Nutmeg - a light grating
- Rum - 100ml

- Blend together the butter, sugar and nutmeg until you have a smooth mixture.
- Gradually add the rum, beating well after each addition. Taste as you mix until you have the right flavour for you.

Rhubarb Butter

As kids we often dipped raw allotment-grown rhubarb in sugar or ate it like this on brown bread or toast. The sugar here is just to take off the sharp edge.

- Rhubarb - 500g
- White sugar - 120g
- Fresh lemon juice - 1 tbs

- Rinse the rhubarb, slice it into 2cm pieces and put in a heavy bottomed saucepan with the sugar. Add the lemon juice, plus about 2 tbs of water and stir to combine.
- Heat, stirring constantly, until the rhubarb juice begins to run and the mixture comes to a boil. Simmer gently for about 20-30 minutes, until the rhubarb is very soft and broken down.
- Purée the mixture in a blender, be careful—hot liquids scald!
- Put the purée in a clean saucepan and bring to a boil, then lower the heat and let it gently bubble away at least 20 minutes until reduced and thickened to your liking. Stir often so it doesn't scorch.
- Spoon the finished butter into a glass jar. Let cool, then cap and refrigerate. It will thicken further as it cools.

BREAD

They say if you ever want to sell a house you should bake bread the day potential buyers are coming to view it. Certainly, one of the most comforting culinary smells has to be fresh bread. The most famous bread of the Northern Counties is probably Stottie Cake—although it's not a cake at all. It's also known as oven-bottom bread and flatty. But there are others that are rarely found elsewhere in the country, including fadge—a small loaf that comes in a variety of shapes, and batten bun—a sort of short baguette perfect to hold a long sausage.

Bread Glaze

Gives all your bread a polished finish that looks very professional.

- Cold water - 4 tbs
- Cornflour - ½ tsp

- Whisk cornflour and water together in a small saucepan and heat till it begins to boil.
- Lower heat to simmer and whisk constantly until thickened and opaque.
- Brush on bread or rolls about 10 minutes before the baking time is up, and then again about 3 minutes before bread comes out of the oven.

Best White—Makes 2 large loaves

- Strong white flour - 1kg
- Milk - 750ml
- Active dry yeast - 7g
- Sugar - 2 tsp + 2 tsp
- Salt - 2 tsp
- Large eggs - 3 lightly beaten
- Unsalted butter - 125g softened

- Heat 180ml of milk to lukewarm, pour into a medium bowl and sprinkle in the yeast. Let stand until the yeast dissolves and the milk becomes creamy and starts to bubble, about 5 minutes.
- Stir in 180g of the flour. Cover with plastic wrap and let the sponge rise about 20 minutes.
- Scrape the sponge into a large bowl and add the sugar, salt, butter, eggs and the remaining milk and mix until blended.
- Gradually add the remaining flour, then continue to knead until the dough is very soft and silky, about 10 minutes longer.
- Transfer the dough to a lightly buttered bowl and cover with a sheet of oiled plastic wrap. Let the dough stand in a warm place until doubled in bulk, about 1 hour.

- Punch down the dough, then cover and let it rise until doubled in bulk again, about 1 hour longer.
- Punch down the dough again and turn it out onto a heavily floured work surface.
- Divide the dough in half and let rest on a lightly-floured work surface for 20 minutes.
- As it rests, preheat the oven to 190°C.
- When risen, shape into loaves and gently ease them into two large, well-buttered loaf pans.
- Cover the pans loosely with oiled plastic wrap and let stand in a warm place until the dough rises well above the rims, about 45 minutes.
- Bake at 190°C for 25 minutes.
- Glaze the loaves.
- Let the bread cool completely on wire racks before slicing.

Best Brown

There's something so comforting and homely about brown bread and it's a testimony to simplicity that it can put to shame many a gourmet feast. Use newly-bought flour to be sure of a clean fresh taste.

- Water - 335ml
- Vegetable oil - 60ml
- Eggs - 2 beaten
- Salt - ½ tsp salt
- Brown sugar - 80g
- White flour - 284g
- Whole wheat flour 142g
- Multigrain flour - 155g
- Active dry yeast - 7g

- Place water in large mixing bowl and add sugar, and yeast.
- When mixture has started to bubble, add eggs, oil and gradually add in salt and flour, mixing well, first with a large metal spoon and then using your hands.
- Mix and knead really well, using a little extra flour as you go to stop it sticking.

- Knead until smooth and sticky, but not sticky enough to cling to surface.
- Place in warm, greased bowl and cover.
- Allow to rise for two hours or so until doubled in volume.
- Punch down dough and knead lightly.
- Shape into 2 loaves and place in greased loaf pans.
- Cover and allow to rise for at least one more hour.
- Bake at 190°C for 25 minutes.
- Glaze the loaves.
- Cool completely on baking rack before slicing.

Brown George

This fadge is an old style that has made a recent come-back with the home bakers. It was the early move away from heavier brown breads toward lighter loaves. Eventually the barley was replaced with white flour to make a lighter but still nutritious bread. Recipe comes from Wensleydale.

- Wholemeal flour - 1kg
- White flour - 450g
- Salt - 1 tsp
- Lard - 30g melted
- Bicarbonate of soda - 1 tbs
- Cream of Tartar - 1.5 tsp
- Milk and water combined - 1 litre

- Mix the flours together with the cream of tartar.
- Mix the bicarbonate of soda in a little milk and add to it the melted lard, then add the rest of the milk.
- Mix the wet ingredients into the dry and form a dough.
- Shape into small flattish loaves and bake in preheated 190°C oven until a toothpick inserted into the centre of the loaf comes out clean, 45-50 minutes.

Shildon Bannocks

An example of an oatmeal soda bread from times before wheat flour became cheaply available. This was probably baked right in front of an open fire, which shows it is a very old recipe. A griddle is the traditional method of cooking, but they can also be baked in a 180°C oven.

- Oatmeal - 115g
- Dripping - 1 tbs melted
- Bicarbonate of soda - ½ tsp
- Salt - ½ tsp
- Hot water to mix

- Put the soda, salt and dripping into a well in the oatmeal and mix to a stiff dough with hot water.
- Knead until it no longer sticky, then roll out thin.
- Bake on hot griddle, flipping half way through.

Eat well-buttered while warm.

Pot Cob—Makes 1 large round loaf

A heavy pot with a tight-fitting lid is required for this old-style bread. I'm guessing it used to be baked in a Northumbrian yetlan pan—a three-legged cauldron pot that dangled from a hook above an open fire. I have included this no-knead recipe, which would have been made before ovens, and would be what is these days called a sourdough, which is how bread was once made with wild yeast and beneficial bacteria. Such bread was (and does) have a local signature making it unique to whichever area it is made. Be sure to use a mild-flavoured beer such as light lager as you don't want the bitterness of hops coming through. This bread is best eaten the day it is baked, but will keep for two more days if wrapped well and stored in a cool place.

- Plain flour - 350g
- Active dry yeast - 7g
- Salt - 1½ tsp
- Water - 180g plus 2 tbs
(continued over page)

- Mild-flavoured beer - 60ml plus 2 tbs
- White vinegar - 1 tbs

- Mix flour, yeast, and salt in large bowl.
- Add water, beer, and vinegar and fold together to form a ball. Cover bowl with plastic wrap and let sit at room temperature for 8-18 hours.
- Transfer the dough to a lightly floured work surface and knead 10-15 times.
- Shape dough into ball by pulling edges into middle. Transfer dough, seam-side down, to parchment-lined heavy pot and spray surface of dough with cooking spray.
- Cover loosely with plastic wrap and let rise at room temperature until dough has doubled in size, about 2 hours.
- About 30 minutes before baking, adjust oven rack to lowest position, place 6- to 8-litre heavy-bottomed pot (with lid) on rack, and heat oven to 260°C.
- Lightly flour top of dough and, using razor blade or sharp knife, make one slit along top of dough.
- Carefully remove heated pot from oven and remove lid.
- Lift the ends of the parchment paper and lower the loaf into pot (let any excess parchment hang over pot edge).
- Put the lid on the pot and place in oven.
- Reduce temperature immediately to 220°C and bake covered for 30 minutes.
- Remove lid and continue to bake until loaf is dark brown, about 20 minutes longer.
- Remove bread from the pot, transfer to wire rack and cool completely.

Tricorn Loaf

Good bread is one of life's great pleasures and I always feel a little sorry for those with gluten intolerance who cannot indulge in the glories of a well-made loaf. Before the invention of the oven, most bread in the Northern Counties would have been baked in a yetlan pan over an open fire. The yetlan was a cast iron pot with three legs that could be stood right in the coals or hung from a fireplace crane above the fire. Although the yetlan has long since disappeared from modern kitchens the method of baking has recently been revived and come full circle as something new.

- Water - 270g luke warm
- Salt - ½ tbs
- Sugar - 1½ tbs
- Active dry yeast - 70g
- Whole wheat flour - 90g
- Rye flour - 90g
- White bread flour - 90g
- Plain flour - 300g
- Vegetable oil - 3 tbs

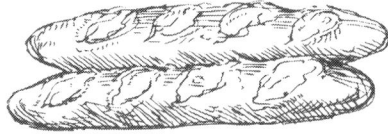

- In a large mixing bowl, combine water, sugar and salt, stir to dissolve.
- Sift the whole wheat flour, rye flour and bread flour with 2 tsp yeast into the water. Whisk together until well blended. Let it rise on the counter uncovered for 3 hours, stirring every hour.
- Using your hands or the dough hook attachment on a kitchen mixer, add the plain flour a handful at a time until well blended, scraping down the bowl if needed.
- Blend in the rest of the flour a little at a time.
- Once all the flour is incorporated, add 2 tbs vegetable oil and let it mix for an additional 20 minutes or until dough no longer sticks to the bowl.
- Let it rise in the bowl, uncovered, until double in volume (about 45 min).
- Grease your bread pans and counter with the vegetable oil and transfer the dough onto the oiled counter.
- Pinch the dough in half.
- Place dough into each prepared bread pan and mold the dough to the base of the pan (no gaps in the corners). Let them rise on the counter until 2½ to 3 times in volume (about 1½ hours).
- Bake at 190°C for 55 minutes.
- Remove loaves immediately from the pans and brush the tops with butter. Cool on a wire rack.

Toasting Bread

What can I say? In the Northern Counties we love toast and it's no surprise we have a recipe dedicated to making a bread that makes great toast. I remember sitting in front of an open fire with a toasting fork made of twisted wire. An exacting job to gauge the doneness of the bread, which differed for each person!

- Active dry yeast - 14g
- Plain flour - 780gs
- Sugar - 450g
- Salt - 2 tsp
- Milk - 475ml
- Bicarbonate of soda - ¼ tsp
- Water - 235ml

- Combine half the flour with yeast, sugar, salt and bicarbonate of soda.
- Pour milk into water and heat until luke warm.
- Add wet mixture to dry mixture and beat well.
- Stir in rest of flour to make a stiff batter.
- Spoon into 2 loaf pans that have been greased and sprinkled with flour. Cover and let rise in warm place for 45 minutes.
- Bake at 200°C for 25 minutes.
- Remove from pans immediately and cool on racks.

Newbiggin Bread

This is a big, blousy, firm-textured and crusty old-fashioned white bread. There are a number of places throughout the Northern Counties, including individual farms, called Newbiggin. The recipe here is direct from the baker who sold this bread from a stall at Hexham market.

- Active dry yeast - 7g
- Warm water - 60ml
- Hot water - 500ml
- Sugar - 3 tbs
- Salt - 1 tbs
- White flour - 800g
- Vegetable oil - 65ml

- Add the yeast to warm water, do not stir. Set aside.
- In a large bowl, pour hot water over the sugar and salt, stir to dissolve, then mix in 400g of flour.
- Pour the oil on top of the dough mixture then add the yeast mixture on top (don't stir it yet). Add the remaining 400g of flour and mix well.
- Cover the bowl with a damp towel and let rise for a minimum of 45 minutes and up to 2 hours.
- Divide the dough in half and knead for a few minutes.
- Flatten each half into a roughly rectangular shape, about 2cm thick, then roll up the dough lengthwise and place on one large or two regular sized floured baking sheets. Cover with moist towel and allow to rise again for at least another 45 minutes.
- After the dough has risen a second time, slash the top of each loaf a few times.
- Bake in a preheated oven at 180°C for 25 minutes.
- Glaze the bread (page 170).
- Allow to cool completely before slicing.

Batten Bread—Makes 2 loaves

Battens are perfect for long lengths of Cumberland sausage.

- Plain flour - 160g
- Active dry yeast - 7g
- Warm water - 100ml
- Salt - 1 tsp

- Mix flour and yeast. Add the water and mix for one minute. Add the salt and knead for another 15 minutes.
- Put the dough in a bowl, cover with a piece of cloth and leave it to rise in a warm place for 20 minutes. Pre-heat oven to 240°C.
- Divide the dough into two pieces shaped like sausages and place on a baking sheet.
- Cover with a cloth and leave them to rise for another 10 minutes. With a sharp knife, cut 3-4 diagonal slashes on the battens.

- Bake for 30 minutes. If you want a shiny, crisp crust, glaze the battens during baking (page 170).

Barley Batten: Use half white flour, half barley flour. Proceed as with batten bread.

Black Batten: Use ¾ white flour, ¼ rye flour. Proceed as with batten bread.

Ramson Loaf—Makes 2 loaves

This is a little bigger than Batten bread but with the added flavour of wild garlic. I couldn't figure out this bread until I discovered that 'ramson' is a very old word for wild garlic. I had previously thought it a type of berry! It makes sense now … You may substitute chives for the wild garlic but it will not be the same. If you use ordinary garlic, make sure you use only about a teaspoon of juice and not the chopped cloves, unless you really like garlic!

- Plain flour - 160g
- Active dry yeast - 7g
- Warm water - 100ml
- Salt - 1 tsp
- Bunch wild garlic chopped fine*

Pre-heat the oven to 240°C

- Mix flour and yeast. Add the water and mix for one minute. Add the salt and the wild garlic and knead for another 15 minutes.
- Put the dough in a bowl, cover with a piece of cloth and leave it to rise in a warm place for 20 minutes.
- Divide the dough into two pieces shaped like cigars and place on a baking sheet. Cover with a cloth and leave them to rise for another 10 minutes.
- With a sharp knife, cut 3-4 diagonal scars on the battens. Bake for 30 minutes. If you want a crisper crust, give the battens an egg-wash just before baking.

*obviously, the more wild garlic the more distinct the flavour.

Castle Eden Salt Buns—Makes 12 rolls

- Milk - 180ml heated to 45°C
- Active dry yeast - 7g
- 1 tsp malt syrup - 1 tsp
- Plain flour - 480g
- Coarse salt - 1½ tsp
- Unsalted butter - 35g cut into 1cm cubes, softened
- Coarse salt for sprinkling

- Mix milk, yeast and malt syrup in a large bowl let sit until foamy.
- In a medium bowl, whisk together flour and salt, add to milk mixture along with butter and stir until a dough forms.
- Transfer to lightly floured work surface and knead until smooth.
- Place in a lightly greased bowl, cover with plastic wrap and leave until doubled in size, about 1 hour. Punch down dough, then cover and allow to rise again, about 45 minutes.
- Heat oven to 160°C.
- Shape dough into a dozen balls, about 40g each, and transfer to a greased 20 x 20cm baking pan, nestling them side by side; cover loosely with plastic wrap and let them double in size, about 2 hours. Brush with clarified butter and bake until puffed and pale golden brown, 20–22 minutes.
- Transfer to a rack and brush with more clarified butter; sprinkle each roll with a small pinch of coarse salt and serve warm.

Threshing Day Bread

This scone-like bread used to be baked on a griddle and made when the new barley was being threshed. It is still the custom on some Northumberland farms to make this bread for family and visitors during harvest time.

- Barley flour - 450g
- Plain flour - 110g
- Salt - 1 tsp
- Bicarbonate of soda - 1 tsp
- Cream of tartar - 2 tsp

(continued over page)

- Buttermilk or milk - 600ml
- Beaten egg - a little

Preheat oven to 240°C.

- In a bowl, mix together the flours, salt, bicarbonate of soda and cream of tartar.
- Stir in the milk to form a firm dough.
- Turn out on to a lightly floured surface and form into a round scone shape about 2cm thick.
- Place on a lightly greased baking sheet and bake for 20 minutes, glazing after 10 minutes.
- Allow to cool completely and serve with best butter.

Durham Pikelets

Durham pikelets differ from others by having no egg, which can make the pikelet dense. They are lighter and slightly sweet, and very similar to the breakfast pancakes of North America.

- Plain flour - 250g
- Buttermilk to mix (about 225ml)
- Sugar - 40g
- Baking powder - 2 tsp
- Salt - a pinch

- Mix the flour, baking powder and the salt.
- Make a well in the centre of the dry mixture and pour in enough buttermilk to form a batter. Drop large spoonfuls into frying pan and fry gently till brown on both sides. Serve hot with butter.

Felton Spice Loaf

The little priest of Felton
The little priest of Felton
Caught a mouse
Within his house
And no one there to help him.

- Butter - 110g
- Sugar - 110g
- Eggs – 2
- Ground almonds - 50g
- Self raising flour - 110g
- Mixed spice - ½ tsp
- Candied peel - 50g chopped fine
- Sultanas - 175g
- Milk - a little

Preheat oven to 190°C.

- Cream the sugar and butter together in a bowl until light and fluffy, then beat in eggs one at a time. Fold in the ground almonds.
- Sift together the flours and mixed spice and fold into the mixture.
- Stir in the peel and sultanas and add sufficient milk to give a soft dropping consistency.
- Turn the mixture into a well-buttered roasting tin, and smooth the surface. Bake for 30-40 minutes.
- Cool for 5 minutes in the tin, then turn out on to a wire rack.
- Serve sliced, plain or very lightly buttered.

Durham Parkin

What Northern cookbook would be complete without a Parkin recipe? Durham's parkin is a little lighter than most because it uses golden syrup instead of treacle.

- Fine oatmeal - 500g
- Baking powder - 2 tsp
- Lard - 120g
- Ground ginger - 2 tsp
- Mixed spice - 1 tsp
- Golden syrup - 250g

- Rub lard into oatmeal and mix in the spices and baking powder.
- Warm the syrup and mix it into the oatmeal till you have a stiff mixture.
- Grease a flat baking tin, pour in the parkin and bake for 1 to 1¼ hours at 150°C.

Singin' Hinnies

These wedges cut from a large scone are one of the more famous traditions of Tyneside. They say the name comes because they 'sing' as they cook. Mine have all been mute. Made in smaller rounds, they are also known as Northumberland Girdle Cakes and Gosforth Griddies.

- Plain flour - 225g
- Salt - a pinch
- Baking powder - 1 tsp
- Butter - 50g
- Lard - 50g
- Sugar - 25g
- Currants or sultanas - 75g
- Milk - 2-3 tbs

- Sift flour, salt and baking powder together in a bowl, then rub in the butter and lard until the mixture resembles fine breadcrumbs.
- Stir in the sugar and fruit and mix to a stiff dough with the milk. Roll into a ball, then turn out on to a lightly floured surface and flatten into a round cake about 1cm thick.

- Lightly grease and heat a frying pan or griddle and put the hinny into it. Prick the top lightly with a fork and cook for 15-20 minutes, turning once, until golden brown on both sides.
- Serve hot, cut into wedges and spread with butter.

Nodding Cake

'A Nodding cake can be baked on a girdle or in the oven. The main thing is to make a big round and prick it all over to prevent it ballooning up in the middle. The name is a corruption of kneading (rubbing lard into flour with the hands). Lard or butter in a cake is spoken of as 'nedding' in Northumberland'—Peggy Hutchinson 'North Country Cooking Secrets' 1935

- Lard 225g
- Plain flour 575g
- Baking powder 1½ tsp

- Rub the lard into the flour until the mixture is as fine as meal.
- Add the baking powder and salt and make into a dough with cold water. Roll out quickly, prick with a fork and bake at 200°C for 20 minutes.
- When cooked, cut into squares. Slip a knife through the middle and spread with blackcurrant jam. These were haytime cakes at Stampfordham (Northumberland).

Curranty-doo

"This is fine cut in slices and buttered." – again, from the intrepid Peggy Hutchinson, who travelled around the North collecting farmhouse recipes. It presumes you have already made dough for white bread.

- Bread dough - 450g
- Lard - 50g
- Sugar - 100g
- Currants - 175g

- Cut the dough off the bulk when it is ready for kneading for tins.
- Spread it out flat on the pastry board.
- Put bits of lard all over it, then sprinkle with sugar and currants.

- Work all of it into the paste until it is evenly distributed, then knead lightly into loaf form, put into a bread pan to rise as for bread, and bake in the usual way.

Fat Rascals

Similar to Singin' Hinnies but with citrus peel and spices. These come from the North York Moors area and were traditionally baked over turf embers inside cast iron pots with heavy lids—the lids were also covered with burning turf.

- Egg - 1 lightly beaten
- Plain flour - 300g
- Baking powder - 2tsp
- Salt - ¼ tsp
- Cold butter - 130g cubed
- Caster sugar - 90g
- Grated orange zest - 1 orange
- Grated lemon zest - 1 lemon
- Ground cinnamon - 1 tsp
- Nutmeg - ½ tsp freshly grated
- Mixed dried fruit (currants, raisins cranberries etc.) - 150g
- Milk - 80ml

Glaze:
- Medium egg yolk, 1 tbs water and a pinch of salt

- Sieve the flour and baking powder into a large bowl. Add the butter and rub in until the mixture resembles fine breadcrumbs.
- Add the sugar, citrus zests, spices and dried fruit and mix well. Add the beaten egg and enough milk (about 50ml) to bring the mixture together into a soft dough. Form the mixture into 6 large scones about 2cm deep.
- Mix the egg yolk, water and salt together to make a glaze and brush this over each rascal.
- Transfer to a non-stick baking tray and bake in a preheated 200°C oven for 15-20 minutes or until golden brown.
- Fat rascals are good served warm from the oven but they can be reheated in a low oven. Serve as they are or with plenty of butter.

Northumberland Twists—Makes 30-36

Twists are yeast-dough strips, twisted, brushed with sherry, sprinkled with sugar and baked. Best eaten warm.

- Strong plain flour - 450g
- Caster sugar - 50g plus extra for sprinkling
- Butter - 110g melted
- Warm water - 150ml
- Active dry yeast - 7g
- Sherry - 3 tbs

- Mix 2 tbs warm water with the yeast and leave to stand for a few minutes until frothy.
- Combine the flour and sugar in a bowl, add the melted butter and mix well.
- Add yeast mixture and the remainder of the water to the flour and mix to a dough.
- Turn out onto a lightly floured surface and knead until smooth and elastic.
- Form into a ball, place in a bowl and cover with a clean tea towel. Leave in warm place for 1½ hours until doubled in bulk.
- Turn the dough out on to a lightly floured surface and knead well, then roll out and cut into strips approximately 10cm long and 1cm wide.
- Twist each strip slightly into a spiral and divide between two well-greased baking sheets. Brush the twists with sherry and sprinkle with caster sugar, then bake in a preheated 190°C oven for 20-25 minutes until golden.

Braided Egg Bread

This strikingly beautiful loaf usually makes an appearance on Easter Sunday, but there is no reason it should not be made more often. When it is made especially for Easter, a few strands of saffron may be steeped in the water to give the bread a beautiful golden hue. This version uses an electric hand mixer but of course you can mix it by hand if you prefer.

- Bread flour - 540g, divided
- Active dry yeast - 7g
- Saffron infused water - 285ml
- Sugar - 50g
- Butter - 60g
- Salt - 1 tsp
- Egg - 1 large, lightly beaten
- Butter - 2 tbs melted

- Combine ¾ of the flour and the yeast in a large bowl.
- Combine water, sugar, butter and salt in medium saucepan. Heat until warm and butter is almost melted.
- Add butter mixture and egg to flour mixture. Beat at low speed of electric mixer 30 seconds, scraping bowl constantly. Beat at high speed 3 minutes. Stir in enough remaining flour by hand to make a soft dough. Shape into a ball.
- Place dough in an oiled bowl, turning to coat surface. Cover. Let rise in warm place 1 hour or until double in size.
- Punch down the dough, place on floured surface and knead until it is no longer sticky.
- Divide the dough in half. Divide each half into thirds. Roll each portion into a 30 x 50cm rope or strand.
- Coat a baking sheet with no-stick cooking spray. Braid three strands together to form a loaf directly on the pan, making sure ends of braided loaf are turned under securely. Repeat with remaining dough.
- Cover and leave the loaves to rise in warm place 1 hour or until double in size.
- Heat oven to 180°C. Bake 15-20 minutes or until golden brown. Brush lightly with melted butter or glaze with egg-wash.

Stotties

Also known as Stotty-cake, flatties, and oven-bottom bread, these fabled loaves are popular for sandwiches with traditional fillings like ham and pease pudding, pork and stuffing or cheese and raw onion. There are many recipes for this bread, but basically it is a short-rise dough that makes a short-baked bread.

Wet:
• Water - 850ml slightly warm
• Active dry yeast - 14g
• Sugar - 1 tsp

Dry:
• Milk powder - 30g
• Plain white flour - 1.5kg
• Salt - 30g
• Sugar - 14g
• Lard - 70g

- In a cup, mix the yeast with a little of the warm water and a pinch of sugar and allow it to foam.
- Sieve all dry ingredients together in a large bowl, then rub in the lard.
- Add the yeast mixture and the water and mix thoroughly.
- Knead for 10-15 minutes, cover with a cloth and let it stand for 30 minutes in a warm place.
- Punch down the dough and pull it into three equal pieces, shape each into a round ball and allow to stand for 10 minutes.
- Roll each ball out to a 22cm circle, cover & leave in a warm place for 20 minutes.
- Place Stotties on a baking tray. Bake in a hot oven 230°C.
- Turn the Stotties over after 8 minutes. Tradition requires you press a hole in the middle of each to deflate them.
- When light brown both sides (about 20 minutes) they're done.
- You can set them to cool completely, but they are also good warm from the oven.

Cathedral Scones

Any visit I make to Durham Cathedral, arguably the most stunning building in the world, ends with a cup of tea and a scone in the café downstairs. I used to have them with strawberry jam and cream but now I just slather them in butter.

- Plain flour - 250g
- Baking powder - 4 tsp
- Salt - ½ tsp
- White sugar - 50g
- Butter - 85g at room temperature
- Milk - 160ml
- Large egg - 1

Preheat the oven to 220°C.

- Combine the flour, baking powder, salt, and sugar in a bowl.
- Add the butter and rub in until completely distributed—the mixture should have a sandy texture to it.
- In a small bowl, whisk together the milk and egg. Set aside 2 tbs for egg wash later, and pour the rest into the bowl with the dry ingredients and stir until a rough dough forms.
- Transfer to a lightly floured countertop and knead about a dozen times until the dough comes together into a relatively smooth ball. Do not to knead too much, or the dough will be tougher and not rise as high.
- Roll the dough about 75 mm thick and use a 75mm cutter to cut about 6 scones. Re-roll the scraps and cut out another.
- Place the scones onto a parchment paper lined or non-stick baking sheet and brush the tops with the reserved egg wash.
- Bake the scones for 13-15 minutes, until well risen and golden brown on the tops and bottoms.

PANTRY SHELF

The pantry in our small terraced house in a mining village had stone shelves and was built into the north wall. That meant it was always cold in there, even in the heat of Summer. Dry goods such as flour and rice and other heavy items were kept there on the lower shelf, and commonly accessed foods like cheese and milk occupied the middle shelves, while long-term items such as spices, sauces and alcohol were kept on the top shelf, out of the reach of children ... and that made the pantry all the more of an Aladdin's Cave.

DRINKS

Finchale Liqueur

I love this drink, not only because it tastes great but because of the shaggy-dog story that came with the recipe—I was told that originally it arrived in a dream to the resident hermit at Finchale Priory in County Durham who made the whisky from scratch and sweetened it with honey. The priory closed in 1535.

- Scotch whisky - 750ml
- Fresh rosemary - 1 sprig
- White sugar - 200ml
- Water - 100ml

- Put the sprig of rosemary into the bottle of Scotch whisky and steep for four days. Discard the rosemary.
- Make a simple syrup by boiling the sugar for about 20 minutes with the water.
- When the syrup is quite cold add the whisky to it. You should end up with about 250ml more than you can fit back into the bottle. Hmm … what to do, what to do?

Softley Gin

So-called because it's where I was given the recipe by a Mr. Teasdale one day when I was cleaning up my great grandparent's grave at St. John's church, Lynesack and Softley. At the time the old schoolhouse was occupied by the Butterknowle Brewery. The talk got around to home brew …

- Eating apples - 250g
- A bit of cinnamon stick
- Whole cloves - 2
- Gin - 475ml
- White sugar -180g
- Water - 120ml

- Core the apples but do not peel. Cut each apple into eight.
- Combine apples, cinnamon stick, cloves, and gin in a large jar.
- Cover with a lid and let steep in a cool, dark place for 2 weeks.
- Strain and filter liquid.
- Make a simple syrup by boiling the sugar for 20 minutes with the water.
- When the syrup is quite cold add it to the filtered gin.
- Pour into bottles and cap tightly.
- Age a minimum of 1 month before serving.

St. Oswald's Celtic Cream

To be truly authentic, the recipe requires gorse flower essence made by steeping the bright yellow flowers of the whin bush in alcohol. Broom flowers do not give the same flavour so do not substitute. Substituting coconut extract is OK because it's not really extracted from coconuts but is a chemical compound that smells like coconut. Gorse flower essence is very similar to coconut and will give a similar flavour when mixed with all the other ingredients.

- Scotch whisky - 450ml
- Evaporated milk - 400g tin
- Condensed milk - 400g tin
- Instant coffee - 1 tsp
- Vanilla extract - ½ tsp
- Coconut extract - ½ tsp

- Dissolve the coffee in the whisky, then add everything else and mix well and consume. Keep it in the fridge, it will go off if left too long. It never has time in my house!

Elderberry Wine

Many modern books on the subject of winemaking belittle so-called country wines and they seem have fallen out of favour to a large extent. However, some old recipes use these old-fashioned wines and before travels to sunnier climes introduced us to the wines of France and Italy, we were happy to make our own from the fruits of the hedgerow. My father made elderberry and blackberry wine each year, although he didn't care for dry wine and his was always sweet. For special occasions he fortified the elderberry with a little brandy and sweetened it further to make what he called 'port.' The recipe below works for just about any berry. If you don't have the space or inclination to make wine from scratch, I suggest you boil a few handfuls of elderberries in a very small amount of water and add the resulting juice to a bottle of store bought dry red wine. You can also use flavoured syrup, the advantage of which is that they contain chemicals that prevent refermentation, although these syrups are almost always cloyingly sweet so be judicious.

- Fresh elderberries - 1kg, or
- Dried elderberries - 225g, or
- Elderberry concentrate - 30ml + 30ml red grape concentrate
- Campden tablet - 1
- Water - 3.75 litres
- Sugar - 1kg
- Citric acid, tartaric acid, yeast nutrients, tannin - 1 tsp of each
- Pectic enzyme - 1 packet
- Dried wine yeast - 30g

- Put the fruit (or concentrate) in a sterilized pail.
- Bring 1 litre of water to the boil and pour into the pail. Add the Campden tablet, leave for 24 hours then mash to a pure. Add the sugar and remaining water, boiling. Stir until the sugar dissolves.
- When cool, add the pectic enzyme and yeast according to the instructions on the packets. Cover the pail with a lid or clean tea-towel and leave in a warm place (about 25°C) for 4 days, stirring once a day.
- Strain into a 4-litre glass fermentation jar, and top up with cooled boiled water if necessary. Fit an airlock and return to the warm place.
- When the gravity has dropped to 1000, or the wine tastes dry, it is ready to filter and bottle.

Remember, this wine is for NEXT year ... patience!

Geordie's Ginger Beer

My dad's recipe. This ginger beer is alive and potentially dangerous if it gets warm ... kind of a wet grenade ... store it in the refrigerator!

- Water - 4 litres boiling
- White sugar - 450g
- Large lemons - 2 juice, pulp and zest
- Fresh root ginger - 100g sliced thin
- Dry yeast - 5g (½ tsp)

- Place the ginger, sugar, and lemons in a large bowl or fermenting pail.
- Pour in the boiling water and stir until sugar dissolves.
- Cover with a cloth and leave for 24 hours.
- Stir the ginger beer and add yeast. Ferment for about one week.
- Strain through a non-metallic sieve or strainer.
- Pour the ginger beer into sound, clean beer bottles and cap with proper beer crowns. Leave them for 4 days before drinking.

CHEESE MAKING

Dales Cheese

Cheese making is a simple, but not necessarily easy thing. The North of England has a long tradition in cheese making and proof of its prowess in world famous names like Cheshire and Wensleydale. I include some cheeses that would have been commonly made at many farms in the region and are fairly easy to reproduce at home. If this is beyond you, rejoice that we have excellent cheesemakers in the Northern Counties and Weardale, Wensleydale, Teesdale and Northumberland produce some of the best in the world.

White Cheese

My Mam taught me how to make this cheese, although when I first tried it myself I was very young and made only about a teacupful so she would not notice the missing milk. I remember what I ended up with was very vinegar-ish, but I have since mastered this easiest of cheeses. It's such a simple cheese to make and tastes so fresh and good you won't mind the effort involved. As a matter of fact, you can make it in a microwave oven almost effortlessly.

Use either goat or cow milk for this cheese—my grandfather had a liking for goat milk and my father did not, so we got very little of it at home and I grew up believing it was somehow strange. Goat milk makes excellent cheese for salads and to spread on crusty bread to go with wine or a pint of best bitter. Cow milk is milder and makes an excellent base for cheesecake (see page 126).

You can use as much milk as you like—but 4 litres is about as much as you can fit into a microwave. If you're using a big saucepan, use as much milk as it will safely hold and increase the vinegar accordingly. Do NOT use an aluminium pan as the acidic vinegar reacts with it and may produce a metallic off-flavour. If using a microwave method, use a food-safe ice-cream pail or similar that will hold all the milk and allow you to use the built-in thermometer.

- Fresh whole milk - 4 litres
- White vinegar - 50ml

- Warm the milk slowly to 60°C (no higher), and maintain that temperature for 10 minutes, stirring to keep it from scorching.
- Slowly add the vinegar. Keep stirring until the curd separates from the whey. It will look like fine, white particles floating in the whey. Then pour it into a cheesecloth-lined colander. Put the colander over another pot to catch the whey for later use.
- Tie the corners of the cloth together and hang to drain over a sink for a few hours. Refrigerate after it has drained. You can add herbs, fruits, finely-chopped chives—anything you want really. I like to divide it up and press it into convenient smaller truckles and roll them in poppyseeds. It will keep for a couple of weeks.

Eldon Blue

- Whole milk - 8 litres
- Whipping cream - 500ml
- Calcium chloride - 5ml
- Mesophilic starter culture (plain organic yoghurt) - 60ml
- Penicillium roqueforte - 0.5ml (or 5g blue cheese mixed to paste with milk)
- Rennet - 5ml
- Salt - 15g

- Heat milk and cream to 30°C, add cultures and calcium chloride and hold at 30°C for 90 minutes. Add rennet and leave till it sets, about 20 minutes.
- Cut curd with whisk very gently and let rest for 30 minutes.
- Pour off whey till just over curd and let rest for 30 minutes more.
- Dip or pour curds into cheesecloth-lined colander or tub. Form cheesecloth into a bag and hang to drain for 15 minutes.
- Press bag of curds between boards with a 4kg weight for 2 hours.
- Return the curds to the pot and break into walnut-sized pieces. Add 15ml salt and mix thoroughly.
- Put curds into 10cm mould and set aside to drain and compress by its own weight. Invert mould several times a day for seven days until the cheese slides out and retains its shape.
- To ripen, it should be in a cool and humid environment. A plastic box with the lid on, kept at around 16°C for a month will encourage blue mold. Once surface bluing is obvious, pierce cheese all over with a long sterile needle or bamboo skewer. Place your box in a fridge, which will maintain about 95% humidity.

Ripe at 60 days but keeps getting better with time.

Buttermilk Cheese

Real buttermilk is what remains after butter has been churned from full fat milk. In days gone by it would have been used up by the farms and dairies that produced it. These days, it is made from scratch by adding cheese bacteria directly to milk. Since buttermilk has become widely available in supermarkets, there is no excuse for not having a go at this delicious spreadable cheese. Is has to be the easiest of all cheeses.

• Buttermilk - 1 litre

- Open a 1-litre carton of buttermilk and leave it standing at room temperature for a day or two, by which time it will have become thick and tangy.
- Place a colander or sieve into a larger pan and cover it with cheesecloth or muslin or a sterile close-woven tea towel. Carefully pour in the buttermilk. Let it drain for 24 hours.

- Lift out the cheese, place in another bowl and beat in about 1 tsp of table salt. That's it. You can add fresh herbs at this point, or a little garlic paste to make it more savoury.

Pit Widow's Herb Cheese

Coal mining tragedies occurred far too often and left widows and orphans completely desolate. This simple recipe illustrates the ingenuity of folks in poverty. It differs every time you make it because it comprises whatever cheese that's left over or gone too hard to eat otherwise. Amazingly, it's really very good!

- Take all the cheese in the house that's dried out or otherwise become unappetizing. If it has developed mold, cut it off and give it a quick rinse under cold water.
- Grate all the cheese into a small saucepan, add a tablespoon of butter and a tablespoon of dry sherry and let it all slowly melt.
- When everything is melted, beat in some fresh herbs—whatever you have at hand, dried herbs will also work—and pour the cheese into a small pot, cover and leave to set. Great on crackers.

Baking Soda Cheese

I found this pre-metric recipe hand-written on the end page of a copy of 'Nicholas Nickleby' printed in 1950. I didn't recognize the handwriting as belonging to my mother, and as my dad only ever read gardening magazines and the racing pink, I have to presume it was by a previous and unknown owner of the book. I take as provenance the fact that in this Dicken's novel 'Dotheboys Hall' was based on a workhouse school near Barnard Castle. I made the cheese and what it produces is something very like processed cheese used for cheese slices. If that's your thing, I would suggest just starting with about a 450g block of cheddar cut into small chunks and going from 'add 1 tsp baking soda.'

"Have 3 gallons of milk in a large kettle on the stove with the heat no hotter that the hand can be held at the bottom of the kettle. Let it stand until milk curdles. Pour into cloth and strain off the whey. Let the curds stand 20 minutes. Crumble well. Add 1 tsp baking soda, 8oz butter and let stand 2 hours. Put into a double boiler and add ½ cup cream and 1 tsp salt and cook until thick, about 45 minutes. Pour into mold and let stand 7 days before using."

THINGS THAT DON'T FIT
ELSEWHERE

Every home has a drawer containing all the things that don't belong in another spot. Cups and plates go in assigned cupboards, cleaning materials go on a particular shelf, pots and pans have a home. But other stuff ... odd shaped screwdrivers, batteries, special cloths, adhesive tape, picture hooks and pins ... go into the catchall drawer. Likewise, we have a few things that don't have home in other chapters, but are much loved and needed nevertheless!

Summerhouse Hash

I wasn't quite sure where this belongs as it contains three different proteins plus vegetables. This breakfast plate, however, is so good it definitely belongs somewhere in our traditional collection. This version courtesy of the Bay Horse pub in Heighington, County Durham.

- Poached eggs - 2
- Summerhouse Spicy Sausage (page 97) - 1 cooked and sliced
- Potatoes - 2 medium pan fried
- Mushrooms - three or four sliced thin and fried in butter
- White Cheddar cheese - 60g grated
- Red onion - 1 medium pan fried
- Ground rosemary - ½ tsp (or 1 tsp fresh chopped very fine)
- Salt and pepper - to taste

- Cook the potatoes and red onion in a frying pan.
- Add the cooked sausage and cooked mushrooms and heat through.
- Add the cheese, rosemary and seasoning.
- Top with two poached-as-you-like-them eggs, serve with toast.

Yorkshire Pudding

One of our most famous Northern Counties recipes, which is also difficult to categorize, is Yorkshire pudding. Everybody swears by their family recipe, so here is my grandfather's recipe, taught to him by his mother who lived most of her life in Yorkshire in the 19th century. You may substitute lard or vegetable oil for the dripping.

- Large eggs - 4
- Milk - 250ml
- Water - 100ml
- Salt - ½ tsp
- Plain flour - 300g
- Dripping - 60g

Preheat oven to 230°C

- In a bowl, beat together the eggs, water and milk.
- Gradually add the flour and beat until smooth.
- Stir in the salt and transfer to a jug to facilitate pouring.
- For individual Yorkshires, put a teaspoon of dripping into each section of a Yorkshire pudding pan or muffin pan. For one large pudding, put all the dripping into a roasting pan. Put the pan onto the top shelf of the oven until it gets very hot.
- Remove the pan from the oven and quickly pour in the batter to ¾ fill the cups, (if using a single pan just carefully pour it all in).
- Bake 20-25 minutes until the Yorkshires are well risen and golden brown. Don't open the oven door until they're done.

Berwick Herb Sausages

A very old way to use up leftover oatmeal from both sides of the Border. If you use vegetable bullion powder and fry these in oil you can have a vegan breakfast. I have a non-vegan breakfast of them with a couple of fried eggs when there's porridge left over. If you have a greater or lesser quantity of leftover porridge, simply adjust the other ingredients. You can even make porridge fresh if you wish, but let it go cold before making these.

- Cold porridge - about 250g
- Fresh breadcrumbs - 50g
- Egg - 1
- Bouillon powder - 1 packet
- Dried sage - ½ tsp

- Mix everything together to form a stiff dough.
- Shape into sausages or patties and fry until brown and crisp.

Nettle Syrup

A few curious curatives sent to Farmers Weekly magazine back in 1935 from Miss E. Rutherford, Northumberland, but my advice is if you are ill see your doctor. Nettles are making a bit of a comeback as a home remedy, but be sure to wear gloves when you gather them!

"Gather the tops of young nettles, wash well and to every 1lb. [450g] of nettles add 1 quart [1 litre] of water. Put into a pot and boil for 1 hour. Then strain, and to every pint [475ml] add 1lb. [450g] sugar; boil for 30 minutes, and when cold bottle it up.

This syrup we make from a very old recipe and it is said to have health-giving powers as a blood purifier. Used with soda water it is a cooling drink."

Rose Syrup

"Cut 1lb. [450g] of rhubarb, simmer in 1 pint [475ml] cold water until all juice is extracted, then strain. To this liquid add ¾lb. [350g] white sugar and the petals of seven red roses. Simmer gently for 15 minutes. Strain free of petals and boil until syrup thickens, when it will be a rich red colour. Pour into clean, dry, warmed jars and seal very securely. To make a good drink, put a teaspoonful into a milk beaker and dissolve it in a tablespoonful of boiling water. When cold, fill up with milk. This is an excellent cure for sore throats, and is also a splendid pick-me-up."

Buttercup Ointment

Another verbatim folklore medicine from Northumberland illustrating the need for lotions to sooth rough skin of farm workers and the economic wisdom of making your own.

"Put ½ lb pure vaseline into a pan with as many buttercup flowers (without the stems) as can possibly be pressed into it. Allow to simmer (not boil) for ¾ hour. While still hot, strain through muslin into small pots. It is ready for use when cold, and is very good for skin troubles."

The Grease Pot—once common in Northern Counties kitchens

'Then it required a one-hour round trip to the butcher's shop where we emerged with two types of fat the butcher was happy to give us free—a couple of pounds of very firm beef fat and perhaps half that amount of pork fat.

"This is ordinary trimmings of pork fat, not the good stuff," said Nelson. "The good stuff comes off the pig's back and when it's cooked it stays soft but doesn't melt, so you get those nice white pieces in Summer sausage and black pudding." I liked both those things so I automatically became a supporter of pork back-fat. When we got back home the two fats went into a cast iron pot with a pint of water and were cooked over low heat until the fat rendered—a miraculous process whereby the liquid fat came out of the solid fat, the water evaporated and the result was a soft, almost white fat that was spreadable at room temperature. It didn't end there though—Nelson scooped out the solids that had wizened down into crackling, sprinkled them with salt and pepper, and put them to one side. He added to the clear fat some vegetables—leek, onion, carrot, parsnip, and a little white turnip—all chopped into small cubes. To this he added a pinch of salt, a couple of peppercorns, a fresh bay leaf, and a sprig of fresh thyme, then he left it on the stove for remainder of the day. In the evening as the sun set in gold over the hills far to the west, he strained the fat mixture through a wire sieve and poured the clear fat into the ready and waiting grease pot.

The next morning the grease had solidified into the beautiful and aromatic base of a thousand meals. We often had this spread on bread. Where many other families had dripping only after meat had been roasted, we had this simple and tasty flavouring available all the time … and I think my favourite part was during the process when Nelson sprinkled salt onto the hot cracklings and offered them to me. I could not believe something so simple and cheap could taste so good.'

~ an excerpt from *Singing Stones and Blue Trout*
   — by Philip Atkinson available from Amazon books online

Plating

There's the story of a Geordie visiting, for the first time, an exclusive and highly respected restaurant in Newcastle that proudly served its food in the French manner of *haute cuisine*. He ordered lamb, which arrived at the table extremely rare and positively pink.

"A good vet could have that back on its feet," he told the waiter. Which leads us to ask the question of how food should be served. Well, my answer is a quote from the Bard: 'As you like it.' How can we insist on a singularity of personal taste when it is by definition a subjective issue? It may irk the chef when a guest orders a steak 'well done,' but if that's the way it's liked, the challenge is to serve it as requested and to still provide the best dining experience possible. Presentation—what chefs call 'plating' … that is, how the food looks on the plate—is important in influencing the diner on the quality of the meal overall. It doesn't need to be fancy—just thoughtful enough to show someone cared.

Daddry Tea

The original recipe for this concoction came with instructions for gathering and preparing hazelnuts, which you may certainly do if you know of the whereabouts of a hazelnut tree, but for simplicity's sake I recommend you just buy them.

- Black tea - 450g
- Hazelnuts - 100g
- Vanilla pod - 1

- Crack the hazelnuts into very small pieces, the size of rice grains, and mix with the black tea.
- Place the mixture in a jar, push in the vanilla bean and screw down the lid of the jar.
- Store one month then remove the vanilla bean (keep it for the next batch).
- Make tea by infusing a tablespoon of mix with 250ml of boiling water and allow to steep until it is to your liking.
- Strain, add milk and a little sugar if you wish.

Bibliography

A Kipper with my Tea - Alan Davison 1989

Country Living - Elisabeth Luard 1989

Coming Back Brockens - Mark Hudson 1994

Dora's Notebook - Dora Kelly 1967

English Food - Jane Grigson 1974

Farmhouse Cooking - Peggy Hutchinson 1978

Farmhouse Fare - Farmers Weekly 1935

Farmhouse Kitchen - Dorothy Sleightholme 1971

Fine Old Ales and Barley Wine - Phil Atkinson 2003

Great British Cooking: A Well Kept Secret - Jane Garmey 1981

Great Northern Cookbook - Sean Wilson 2012

North Country Cooking Secrets - Peggy Hutchinson 1935

Old English Cookery - Peggy Hutchinson 1951

Patsy Quinn's Notebook - 1987

Preservation of Food - Olive Hayes 1919

Stotty 'n' Spice Cake: - Bill Griffiths 2006

The Classic 1000 Recipes - Foulsham 1992

The Cookery of England - Elisabeth Ayrton 1974

The Lady's Assistant - Charlotte Mason 1767

The Land that Thyme Forgot - William Black 2005

The New Geordie Dictionary - ed Frank Graham 1987

The Scots Kitchen - Marion McNeill 1929

Tyne Valley Recipes From My Mother's Notebook - Ros Kellock

Yorkshire Fare - Margaret Slack 1979

INDEX

Printed in Great Britain
by Amazon